EXPLORING DIVERSITY THROUGH MULTIMODALITY, NARRATIVE, AND DIALOGUE

Exploring Diversity through Multimodality, Narrative, and Dialogue awakens educators to the ways in which values, beliefs, language use, culture, identity, social class, race, and other factors filter approaches to teaching and expectations for students. Designed as a guide to help educators engage in dialogic interactions, the text articulates a theoretically grounded and research-based framework related to the use of personal narratives as learning tools. Educators are encouraged to consider their own positions, explore topics of diversity and social justice, and identify ways to better address student needs.

Drawing on theories from multiliteracies, multimodality, embodiment, and narrative, chapters are framed around book discussions and the use of personal narrative to define and provide examples of dialogic interactions. Unique to this book is its focus on:

- embodied learning and multimodality, as well as myriad artifacts produced by educators;
- listening, not just dialogic talk;
- writing (both traditional print texts and multimodal composition) that supports dialogic interaction; and
- not merely responding to literature but developing empathic responses to texts, students, and others whose opinions may differ from one's own viewpoints.

The specific techniques and approaches presented can be used within educational and professional development settings to help readers enhance their journey toward greater awareness of others and of their own beliefs and experiences that lead toward social justice for all.

Mary B. McVee is Associate Professor, Literacy, and Director of the Center for Literacy and Reading Instruction, Graduate School of Education, University at Buffalo, SUNY, USA.

Fenice B. Boyd is Associate Professor, Literacy, Graduate School of Education, University at Buffalo, SUNY, USA.

EXPLORING DIVERSITY THROUGH MULTIMODALITY, NARRATIVE, AND DIALOGUE

A Framework for Teacher Reflection

Mary B. McVee and Fenice B. Boyd

Routledge
Taylor & Francis Group

NEW YORK AND LONDON

First published 2016
by Routledge
711 Third Avenue, New York, NY 10017

and by Routledge
2 Park Square, Milton Park, Abingdon, Oxon, OX14 4RN

Routledge is an imprint of the Taylor & Francis Group, an informa business

© 2016 Taylor & Francis

Library of Congress Cataloging-in-Publication Data
McVee, Mary B.
  Exploring diversity through multimodality, narrative and dialogue : a framework for teacher reflection / by Mary B. McVee and Fenice B. Boyd.
    pages cm
  Includes bibliographical references and index.
  1. Communication in education.   2. Teacher-student relationships.
3. Reading.   4. Social justice—Study and teaching.   I. Boyd, Fenice B.
II. Title.
  LB1033.5.M33 2016
  371.102'2 dc23
  2015013740

ISBN: 978-1-138-90105-6 (hbk)
ISBN: 978-1-138-90107-0 (pbk)
ISBN: 978-1-315-70031-1 (ebk)

Typeset in Bembo
by Apex CoVantage, LLC

This book is dedicated to every teacher in any classroom who takes the time to see children and youth for who they are and who they may yet become. And for every teacher who echoes the great storytellers in saying: "You can live many stories; the end is not yet written. The possibilities are open. What story will you imagine?"

CONTENTS

PROLOGUE

I take open-mindedness to be a willingness to construe knowledge and values from multiple perspectives without loss of commitment to one's own values. Open-mindedness is the keystone of what we call a democratic culture. We have learned, with much pain, that democratic culture is neither divinely ordained nor is it to be taken for granted as perennially durable.[1]
Jerome Bruner in *Acts of Meaning*

At the heart of education in many countries lies a profoundly democratic ideal—that all children and youth have a right to learn. A foundational element of schooling is often to prepare children to claim this right and live out the ideal within a just and equitable society. Bruner correctly observes that democracy is not a given, even if it is strongly desired. Current world events seem to bear this out as democratic movements have sometimes descended into civil war and brutality or as populations who seemed to be regaining their rights have experienced renewed violence and restrictions of their human rights. Events in the first decades of the 21st century brought great hope that our world was learning tolerance, welcoming openness, and letting people choose their own path. But wherever openness and tolerance appear to be making inroads, intolerance and fear seem to linger.

We argue that teachers have a unique role to play around developing a civil discourse and fostering habits of mind and engagement that encourage children and youth to participate in dialogue with one another and to help propel us toward a more hopeful and peaceful world. Teachers can and do assist youngsters in learning to engage in close, intellectual readings of multiple texts across the content areas. But teachers themselves are cultural beings influenced by their own lived histories and embodied selves. A teacher's race, gender, socioeconomic class history, mother tongue, ethnicity, and cultural identification *all* influence how teachers view themselves *and* their students.

Our lived experiences are the narratives we tell about others and ourselves. All of us, regardless of where we come from or how enlightened we are, filter our awareness through the narrative structures of lived experience. The challenge is that like a fish in water, we often do not recognize that these structures exist unless something is radically altered. When an experience or encounter disrupts our lived experiences, we find our predictable world and environment upended like a fish suddenly removed from water. This upending often happens naturally as part of our lives, sometimes by design and sometimes by chance—our parents divorce suddenly; we take a job in another country; we fall in love with someone with a different religious or racial background; we adopt a child with special needs; we are diagnosed with a serious illness. Such disruptions often cause a profound displacement. The center of our lives seems to shift, often causing us to question our values, beliefs, and assumptions.

These displacement spaces, while uncomfortable, are places that can promote growth and exploration, and literature can help us to explore them. Alone we can be self-reflexive, but in connection with others, we can engage in dialogue and further reflection. The purpose of this text is to open such a space where, even in moments of profound discomfort, we might continue to engage in listening and learning alongside others as we engage in close readings and thoughtful dialogues around rich texts.

> *Stories are light. Light is precious in a world so dark.*
> —Kate DiCamillo in *The Tale of Desperaux*

Note

1. Bruner, J. (1990). *Acts of meaning*. Cambridge: Harvard University Press.

ACKNOWLEDGMENTS

We would like to thank all of the students who have been part of the Language, Literacy, and Culture class that we have had the privilege of teaching over the years. You inspire us! A special thank you and our admiration and respect to students for giving us permission to share excerpts of talk, writing, or multimodal compositions and for feedback.

We acknowledge the support of many others: Our colleagues in the New Literacy Group at Buffalo. Nancy Bailey and Maria Baldassarre Hopkins who helped with original analysis—who knew this would take so long? Greg, for being there in the beginning; you are greatly missed. Colette Carse for teaching from the first chapter drafts and for conversations too numerous to count. Andrea Tochelli for help with the body biography. Tyler Rinker for editing, comments, and walking in two paradigms. Caroline Flury-Kashmanian for using early drafts with students. Taffy Raphael and Susan Florio-Ruane for introducing us to Book Club and helping us think about literature, language, and culture and for wonderful mentorship. Jim Gavelek for introducing us to all the theories we know and love. Lisa Roof for ever-inspiring multimodal representations, the gifts that keep on giving. Tiffany Nyachae for reading so carefully and thoughtfully and for impassioned margin comments; you are as wonderful as you made us feel. Huda Almumen, Abdul Alshehri, and Nuwee Chomphuchart for consulting on stop signs. Cindy Brock for brilliant feedback (as always) even from down under! Jan, help with images, and the best Chinese food in Buffalo—it's hard to write on an empty stomach. Zach, Jaden, and Lilli because you are the future, and you give us hope! Special thanks to Lillianna Zhang for the awesome cover art.

Partial support for this project came from the Center for Literacy and Reading Instruction (CLaRI) at the University at Buffalo, SUNY, Graduate School of Education.

1
INTRODUCTION

Narrative, Multimodality, and Dialogue in Teaching and Teacher Education

Teachers and teacher educators need opportunities to examine much of what is usually unexamined in the tightly braided relationships of language, culture, and power in schools and schooling. This kind of examination inevitably begins with our own histories as human beings and as educators; our own experiences as members of particular races, classes, and genders; and as children, parents, and teachers in the world.

(Cochran-Smith, 1995, p. 500)

"I never really thought there were poor White people in our city. I just assumed that poor people were Black."

"My family is biracial, and we have people from different cultures in our family, so before this class, I ignored stuff about multiculturalism in my education classes. Because of my background I didn't think I needed to reflect on how my cultural experiences affected my thinking about others or teaching. But it is important for *all* of us to talk about these issues, even me."

"I guess after all these readings about literacy and culture and multimodal projects, I am starting to really understand that race, gender, or economic class do not predict who you will be, but they can shape how people see you and the opportunities you sometimes get access to in the world."

"It's inspiring to hear stories from literacy teachers who really looked at their kids as people with identities and hopes for the future. I want to be that kind of teacher—the one who really listens and tries to understand my students as people and all of the things that students bring with them to school."

These types of comments are typical of the insights that inservice and preservice teachers express during their university coursework as they engage in explorations of language, literacy, and culture in a course that we (Mary and Fenice) have each taught. In a globally connected world where images, music, video, news, and a host of real-time interactive social media vie for our attention, it may seem surprising that these students are not more aware of diverse cultural groups or how their own cultural lenses have shaped their perspectives. After all, any one of us can go online and chat with someone from India, play video games with someone in Australia, use the cloud to co-construct a project about education with someone in China, or watch a weekly podcast produced by African American youth. Yet, we have found in our teaching and research that often many teachers and teacher candidates have not had the opportunity to devote concentrated thought toward understanding various cultural groups and their literacies or even to their own cultural groups and literacies. The need for such explorations is one of the reasons why we wrote this book.

The Purpose of This Book

In this book we present a conceptual framework, along with activities and reflection points, to help teachers and various educational professionals engage in considerations of their own perspectives on literacy, language, and culture. The purpose is to assist all teachers in exploring their beliefs, values, questions, dispositions, and experiences related to diversities. Here, diversities refers generally to mother tongue, economic standing, social class, race, gender, ethnicity, religion and culture, and various forms of literacy.

A major goal of this book is to push readers to explore their own values, beliefs, and expectations for themselves as educators and to explore their expectations for children and youth in society at large and in their own classrooms. Readers will consider how personal beliefs and experiences can influence views of literacy, choice of pedagogical methods and assessments, and ultimately, how such positions affect the lives of children and youth in classrooms by limiting or enhancing learning opportunities.

Assisting teachers in explorations of their own beliefs is critical because many decades of research demonstrates that expectations and attitudes held by educators about what learners can achieve profoundly affects learning in K–12 settings and beyond (cf. Anyon, 1980; Rist, 1970; Scribner, Scribner, & Reyes, 1999; Snow, Barnes, Chandler, Goodman, & Hemphill, 1991; Weis, Cipollone, & Jenkins, 2014). At the same time, there is also research that demonstrates that teacher educators can intervene to positively affect teacher expectations or biases (e.g., Florio-Ruane, 2001; Kumar & Hamer, 2013; Timperley & Phillips, 2003).

Teachers have a pivotal role to play in attempting to address some of the persistent challenges in education. For example, while there has been progress in many countries related to literacy achievement, schooling, and equity, the achievement gap—or what Hilliard (2003) has referred to as the "opportunity gap"—has stubbornly persisted across time, across multiple educational contexts and countries, and disproportionately across particular groups of people (e.g., indigenous peoples, involuntary immigrants, people of color). For democratic societies concerned about social equity and access to equal opportunity, these opportunity gaps are troubling. It is clear that no one solution exists to best create sustained change with regard to the opportunity gap, but regardless of the approach chosen, teachers' beliefs about learners or positions toward them can never be factored out.

One of the key challenges we face in the US, and one that is shared by many other English-speaking countries, is that the demographics of children attending schools have shown a persistent trend. Children entering schools speak many languages other than English, come from multiple economic backgrounds, represent many shades of brown or black, and practice many religions and cultural traditions. At the same time, the cohort of classroom teachers remains white more than brown, more monolingual than multilingual, predominantly middle class, and more female than male. These demographic differences have led teacher educators to consider how to support the development of appropriate pedagogical practices, but also how to help teachers position learners as individuals with rich "funds of knowledge," rather than deficiencies that need to be fixed (Moll, Amanti, Neff, & Gonzalez, 1992). This challenge is at the heart of this book.

Just as teachers are admonished to view children as willing and eager learners possessing specific funds of knowledge, in this text we attempt to present teachers and teacher candidates in a parallel manner. Teachers and teacher candidates are predominantly "competent learners who bring rich resources to their learning" (Lowenstein, 2009, p. 197). At times in this book, readers will see examples of these educators' struggle to connect, to engage, or to explore, but we believe that in all but the rarest exceptions, teachers come to their university classrooms or professional development experiences willing to learn and to build upon whatever funds of knowledge they possess. This book is our attempt to work with teachers in the same respectful but challenging manner in which we would work with children or youth.

We develop our conceptual framework within the Book Club model of adult peer discussion following the work of Florio-Ruane (2001) and Raphael (e. g., Raphael & McMahon, 1994; McMahon, Raphael, Goatley, & Pardo, 1997; Raphael, Pardo, & Highfield, 2002). Book Club serves as a context for **dialogic interactions** to address what we are most concerned about in the literacy and teacher education fields—empowering preservice and inservice teachers to examine and to be better informed about the nexus between literacy, language, and culture. Book Club also provides a framework to enact other practices that are essential to explorations of teaching and learning: personal narrative, dialogic interaction, and multimodal response.

Within our teaching and within this book, **personal narratives**—both published and students' own stories—are valued not only as important but as an essential part of the learning process. Stories are ways in which we create and reshape ourselves (Bruner, 1986, 1990). Stories also defy limiting storylines or what Chimamanda Adichie (2009) refers to as the "danger of a single story" by introducing us to multiple viewpoints. Stories can engage us in dialogic interaction with our peers, characters in texts or even narrators (face-to-face or virtually). These narrators, for example, do not merely rely upon words to convey knowledge, but use multiple modes such as image, sound, gesture, and color (among other modes) to help create meaning. Using multiple modes (i.e., **multimodality**) to respond to texts within a Book Club setting is essential to provide multiple avenues for meaning making and to open up opportunities for exploration and engagement.

The Framework of This Book

Personal Narrative and Dialogic Interaction

In her book *Language, Culture, and Teaching*, Sonia Nieto (2002) noted that it was only recently that language, literacy, and culture became linked in the educational literature. While reviewing the scholarly literature and her own influential work, Nieto described how critical perspectives had often been absent in teacher education, noting:

> . . . until recently, critical perspectives were almost entirely missing from treatments of reading, writing, language acquisition and use, and an in-depth understanding of race, culture, and ethnicity. If broached at all, differences were "celebrated," typically in shallow ways. . . . But discussions of stratification and inequality were largely absent until recently in most teacher education courses. Despite their invisibility questions about equity and social justice are at the core of education. (p. 1)

Nieto used a reflective process similar to the process we hope our students will use. That is, Nieto grounded her introduction to these themes of language, culture, and teaching in her own personal narrative, using her story to illustrate tenets of sociocultural theories of language and learning.

Florio-Ruane (2001) took up this challenge of using narrative to make the less visible trappings of culture visible and to assist teachers in enacting a critical and deep engagement. She described work from a number of research studies in which she conceptualized, implemented, and studied the use of personal narrative and autobiography in Book Club discussions. Teacher participants considered these complex issues of culture, ethnicity, and equity from an ethnographic stance. Through these "ethnographic stories of self" (p. 3), Florio-Ruane found that participants began to explore identities, both their own and others, and to "probe more deeply their own formations and their relationships with others" (p. 5).

Florio-Ruane boldly asserted that when "Viewed this way, telling and reading of stories of culture is not an educational frill. It is activity central to identifying the sources of our identities as Americans and, in the process, of identifying the sources of American inequality" (p. 26).

While this quote speaks directly to the American context, teacher educators and scholars from multiple countries continue to wrestle with how to explore these issues of identity and inequality. For example, consider the following range of studies from traditionally English-speaking countries: Australia (e.g., Allard & Santoro, 2006; Santoro, Kamler, & Reid, 2001), Canada (e.g., Strong-Wilson, 2007), England (e.g., Lander, 2011; Pearce, 2003), Ireland (e.g., Hagan & McGlynn, 2004) and the United States (e.g., McVee, Brock, & Glazier, 2011; Garratt & Segall, 2013).

Unfortunately, more than a decade after these powerful works by Nieto and Florio-Ruane were written, we find that the field of teacher education continues to struggle with how to assist teachers and other educational professionals in dialogic explorations around diversity. Despite the rich array of work that has been conducted in this area of teacher education (cf. Boyd & Brock, 2004; Cochran-Smith, 2004; Cochran-Smith, Davis, & Fries, 2004; Fishman & McCarthy, 2000; Ladson-Billings, 2006; Lowenstein, 2009; Phillon, He, & Connelly, 2005; Rogers, Marshall, & Tyson, 2006), many of our students, even those who have already obtained initial teacher certification, report that they have not been provided with opportunities to deeply explore these inequities at any level of their education journeys. Those who indicate they have been exposed to some notions of multiculturalism suggest that their multicultural curricula were either the shallow celebrations of differences such as festivals, food, and traditions that Florio-Ruane, Nieto, and other scholars caution against, or generalized versions of multiculturalism to which these teacher candidates often found no personal connection.

While these multicultural explorations are perhaps most crucial to White teachers who are working with children from social, economic, linguistic, racial, and ethnic backgrounds that are not considered mainstream, scholars have found that all teachers, regardless of their background, need to explore the ties between their views, schooling, and literacy (e.g., Glazier, 2009; Santoro, 2007).

It is clear that many teacher educators—ourselves included—are still wrestling with how to implement the ideas so eloquently proposed by Nieto, Florio-Ruane, and other scholars. In this text we take up their work by employing personal narratives (Chapter 2) and dialogic interaction (Chapter 5).

Peer-Led Book Clubs for Educators

Although there are many feasible frameworks for exploring considerations of literacy and diversity, we have implemented a Book Club framework as developed by Raphael and her colleagues (Raphael & McMahon, 1994; McMahon et al., 1997) and as adapted by Florio-Ruane and Raphael in explorations of teachers learning about culture through autobiography (e.g., Florio-Ruane, 2001; Florio-Ruane, Raphael, Glazier, McVee, & Wallace, 1997). Chapter 3, coauthored with Taffy Raphael, provides a conceptual and structural overview of elements of Book Club.

Peer-led Book Clubs can be a powerful structure for learning. They allow time and space for students to engage in authentic dialogue and explorations around meaningful texts—their own and others. Texts can easily be adapted for context (e.g., working with teachers in an urban school with a high proportion of new immigrants and refugees; working with teacher candidates in a university-based literacy course; working with administrators and curriculum coaches seeking to lead a district initiative around diversity). More importantly, Book Club allows for dialogic engagement (Chapter 3), personal narrative and reflection (Chapter 2), and multimodal meaning making (Chapter 4). Book Club structures allow teacher educators to guide learning rather than present information in a teacher-directed transmission-oriented approach. Teachers are still very important in guiding, shaping, scaffolding, challenging, exhorting, responding, and critiquing, but participants use their Book Clubs as settings of opportunity to engage in dialogue or what Burbules (1993) has called "activity directed toward discovery and new understanding (p. 8).

Multimodality and Multiliteracies

There are now several decades of work that attempts to document and conceptualize the linkages between language, literacy, and culture. In contrast, only recently have teacher educators begun to focus on multimodal learning, that is, through multiple modes such as image, print text, color, and so on (McVee, Bailey, & Shanahan, 2008; Miller & McVee, 2012). Whether work is described as new literacies (Miller & McVee, 2012), New Literacy Studies (Pahl & Rowsell, 2006), or multiliteracies frameworks (Boyd & Brock, 2015), work around multimodality is often grounded in the seminal article of the New London Group (1996, 2000) (cf. Boyd & Brock, 2015; Leander & Boldt, 2013). Other recent work around multimodality draws heavily from members of the New London Group such as Gunther Kress (2003, 2010), James Gee (1989, 2004), and Bill Cope and Mary Kalantzis (2000, 2012a) who are routinely cited for their respective work on social semiotics, discourses, and design.

The flurry of research around multimodality tends to emphasize elements of design and the design process and use of modes (Jewitt, 2009). In literacy research this work has often focused on visual meaning to the exclusion of other modes such as sound or gesture (cf. Shanahan, 2012; Shanahan & Roof, 2013) and foregrounded design and use of modes over considerations of identity and embodiment (e.g. Burnett, Merchant, Pahl, & Rowsell, 2014; Rowsell & Pahl, 2007). This foregrounding of design, while a necessary aspect of the multimodal composing process, also runs the risk of deemphasizing or neglecting the role of embodied teaching and learning. The term "multimodal design" does more than just suggest embodied perspectives. By their very nature, modes *are* embodied processes. Modes are used as we see, hear, touch, taste, smell, and experience. Embodiment pertains to ways of doing and acting but also ways of feeling, believing, and valuing. Since the rise of Enlightenment rationalism in the 18th century, Western societies have posited a rational mind separated from the body, whereas multimodal composition taps into the ways in which learning itself is grounded in the body (see Chapter 4).

We posit that multimodality brings richness and layers of potential complexity to the dialogue around teachers' concerns about diversity. Furthermore, this connection between multimodality, equity, and diversity is at the heart of multiliteracies. In the opening of their book chapter, the New London Group (2000) assert that a fundamental mission of education:

> is to ensure that all students benefit from learning in ways that allow them to participate fully in public, community, and economic life. Pedagogy is a teaching and learning relationship that creates the potential for building learning conditions leading to full and equitable social participation. Literacy pedagogy, specifically, is expected to play a particularly important role in fulfilling this mission. (p. 9)

From the New London Group's perspective, both elements of design and frameworks for pedagogy play a pivotal role in learning, and this point is often stressed in recent publications that draw from the New London Group. However, and very importantly, the original article by the New London Group (1996), the New London Group chapter (2000), and particularly the book *Multiliteracies: Literacy Learning and the Design of Social Futures* (Cope & Kalantzis, 2000) are framed in broad concerns about global change, equity for all social groups, and democratic citizenship. Cope and Kalantzis describe how the term "multiliteracies" represents multiple means of communication and multiple media and also recognizes the "increasing salience of cultural and linguistic diversity" (p. 5). Kalantzis and Cope (2012b) have continued to reframe their definition of multiliteracies. Their book *Literacies* focuses on the "why," "what," and "how" of literacies, and in that text they press ahead, tightening the connections between social diversity and multimodality.

We revoice this connection between multimodality and multiliteracies first made by the New London Group to make the point that multimodality is more than just a recent trend precipitated by the convergence of digital technologies. One goal of our book is to follow in the footsteps of the New London Group and its members such as Kalantzis and Cope (2012b). That is, in our text we explore both the "what" and the "how" of multiliteracies in teacher education to present conceptual explorations of diversity, narrative, and literacy. But, importantly, we also present scaffolds to assist teacher educators, teacher candidates, and educational professionals in engaging with one another through Book Club and through interactive dialogic and multimodal activities to press on with their learning.

Connections to Contemporary Contexts

Our primary purposes in the text are pragmatic. As outlined in Chapters 2–7, we seek to provide a framework that is useful for practical implication in literacy and multicultural teacher education courses but also a framework that is conceptually rigorous and supported by research. While early chapters focus on introducing the conceptual framework and approach, we also illustrate this approach in action to address some of the issues and challenges that can arise when educators attempt to engage students in exploring multiliteracies through engagement that is multimodal, embodied, and dialogic.

Within a democratic society, educators must prepare students to engage in conversation around issues that are difficult and challenging. In the United States we have been plagued by what Tannen (1998) refers to as the "argument culture," where the focus on talk has become winning a contentious argument at all costs. This contrasts with the values that are at the core of a democratic society in which freedom of speech is valued, but we must also learn to listen to those around us and become empathetic to others' points of view. We take up these issues of listening and dialogue in Chapter 6.

The ideals of reasoned, informed, dialogic argument resonates with the ideals of democratic society, but at the same time they also map onto current educational movements. For example, in the US, the Common Core State Standards emphasize two particular approaches to text that form an integral part of the dialogic Book Clubs in which our students engage. First, participants learn to engage in the process of *close reading*. In preparation for Book Club, participants engage in reading, reinterpreting, and rereading as they create multimodal responses to the texts they have read. As they meet with their group, they may engage in further scrutiny of the text. As participants engage with multiple texts, their own and others, they have the opportunity to develop evidence-based arguments that address themes related to literacy, equity, and diversity. Because the educational challenges that face schools are multifaceted, they eschew easy analysis and require explorations and evidence from a variety of sources for deep examination. In this regard, while teachers are learning about diversity, they can also engage in thoughtful exploration of processes that are also relevant to the students they serve, such as composing multimodally, using evidence-based arguments, and examining texts closely for their richer and more nuanced meanings. These processes are not always intuitive, nor do they come easily. Chapter 7 explores what happens when Book Club participants attempt to engage with contentious or challenging topics that Glazier (2003) has referred to as "hot lava" (p. 76) and how multiple texts and multimodal compositions can contribute to these explorations. In Chapter 8, we extend our own stories that began this book and argue that all of us still have learning to undertake related to the rich diversities that are ever more defining our societies.

While we cannot guarantee that deep learning will result from reading this book and engaging in the activities within it, we are optimistic about the successes we have seen with our own students. The proposed framework, conceptual themes, and activities offer opportunities for authentic, engaged learning to help prepare teachers and educators in examining their own positions to become more effective teachers of *all* children. We invite you to read on, to compose multimodally, to engage dialogically, and to continue the journey with us!

References

Adichie, C.N. (2009, July). The danger of a single story. [Video File]. Retrieved from http://www.ted.com/talks/chimamanda_adichie_the_danger_of_a_single_story

Allard, A.C., & Santoro, N. (2006). Troubling identities: Teacher education students' constructions of class and ethnicity. *Cambridge Journal of Education, 36*(1), 115–129. doi:10.1080/03057640500491021

Anyon, J. (1980). Social class and the hidden curriculum of work. *Journal of Education, 162*(1), 67–92.

Boyd, F.B., & Brock, C.H. (Eds.). (2004). *Multicultural and multilingual literacy and language: Contexts and practices.* New York: Guilford Press.

Boyd, F.B., & Brock, C.H. (Eds.). (2015). *Social diversity within multiliteracies: Complexity in teaching and learning.* New York: Routledge.

Bruner, J. (1986). *Actual minds, possible worlds.* Cambridge, MA: Harvard University Press.

Bruner, J. (1990). *Acts of meaning.* Cambridge: Harvard University Press.

Burbules, N. C. (1993). *Dialogue in teaching: Theory and practice.* New York: Teachers College Press.

Burnett, C., Merchant, G., Pahl, K., & Rowsell, J. (2014). The (im)materiality of literacy: The significance of subjectivity to new literacies research. *Discourse: Studies in the Cultural Politics of Education, 35*(1), 90–103. doi:10.1080/01596306.2012.739469

Cochran-Smith, M. (1995). Color blindness and basket making are not the answers: Confronting the dilemmas of race, culture, and language diversity in teacher education. *American Educational Research Journal, 32*(3), 493–522.

Cochran-Smith, M. (2004). *Walking the road: Race, diversity, and social justice.* New York: Teachers College Press.

Cochran-Smith, M., Davis, D., & Fries, K. (2004). Multicultural teacher education: Research, practice, and policy. In J.A. Banks (Ed.), *Handbook of research on multicultural education* (2nd ed., pp. 931–975). San Francisco, CA: Jossey-Bass.

Cope, B., & Kalantzis, M. (Eds.). (2000). *Multiliteracies: Literacy learning and the design of social futures.* New York: Routledge.

Fishman, S.M., & McCarthy, L. (2000). *Unplayed tapes: A personal history of collaborative teacher research.* New York: Teachers College Press.

Florio-Ruane, S. (2001). *Teacher education and the cultural imagination.* Mahwah, NJ: Lawrence Erlbaum.

Florio-Ruane, S., Raphael, T., Glazier, J., McVee, M., & Wallace, S. (1997). Discovering culture in discussion of autobiographical literature: Transforming the education of literacy teachers. In C.K. Kinzer, K.A. Hinchman, & D.J. Leu (Eds.), *Inquiries in literacy theory and practice, 46th yearbook of the National Reading Conference* (pp. 452–464). Chicago, IL: National Reading Conference.

Garratt, H.J., & Segall, A. (2013). (Re)considerations of ignorance and resistance in teacher education. *Journal of Teacher Education, 64*(4), 294–304.

Gee, J.P. (1989). Literacy, discourse, and linguistics: Introduction. *Journal of Education, 171*(1), 5–25.

Gee, J.P. (2004). *Situated language and learning: A critique of traditional schooling.* New York: Routledge.

Glazier, J.A. (2003). Moving closer to speaking the unspeakable: White teachers talking about race. *Teacher Education Quarterly, 30*(1), 73–94.

Glazier, J.A. (2009). The challenge of repositioning: Teacher learning in the company of others. *Teaching and Teacher Education, 25*(6), 826–834.

Hagan, M., & McGlynn, C. (2004). Moving barriers: Promoting learning for diversity in initial teacher education. *Intercultural Education, 15*(3), 244–253. doi:10.1080/1467598042000262545

Hilliard, A. (2003). No mystery: Closing the achievement gap between Africans and excellence. In T. Perry, A. Hilliard, & C. Steele (Eds.), *Young, gifted, and Black: Promoting high achievement among African-American students* (pp. 131–166). Boston: Beacon.

Jewitt, C. (Ed.). (2009). *The Routledge handbook of multimodal analysis.* London: Routledge.

Kalantzis, M., & Cope, B. (2012a). *New learning: Elements of a science of education* (2nd ed.). New York: Cambridge University Press.

Kalantzis, M., & Cope, B. (2012b). *Literacies.* New York: Cambridge University Press.

Kress, G. (2003). *Literacy in a new media age.* New York: Routledge.

Kress, G. (2010). *Multimodality: A social semiotic approach to contemporary communication.* New York: Routledge.

Kumar, R., & Hamer, L. (2013). Preservice teachers' attitudes and beliefs toward student diversity and proposed instructional practices: A sequential design study. *Journal of Teacher Education, 64*(2), 162–177.

Ladson-Billings, G. (2006). It's not the culture of poverty, it's the poverty of culture: The problem with teacher education. *Anthropology & Education Quarterly, 37*(2), 104–109.

Lander, V. (2011). Race, culture and all that: An exploration of the perspectives of White secondary student teachers about race equality issues in their initial teacher education. *Race, Ethnicity and Education, 14*(3), 351–364. doi:10.1080/13613324.2010.543389

Leander, K., & Boldt, G. (2013). Rereading "A Pedagogy of Multiliteracies": Bodies, texts, and emergence. *Journal of Literacy Research, 45*(1), 22–46. doi:10.1177/1086296X12468587

Lowenstein, K.L. (2009). The work of multicultural teacher education: Reconceptualizing White teacher candidates as learners. *Review of Educational Research, 79*(1), 163–196.

McMahon, S.I., Raphael, T.E., Goatley, V.J., & Pardo, L.S. (Eds.). (1997). *The book club connection: Literacy learning and classroom talk.* New York: Teachers College Press.

McVee, M.B., Bailey, N.M., & Shanahan, L.E. (2008). Using digital media to interpret poetry: Spiderman meets Walt Whitman. *Research in the Teaching of English, 43*(2), 112–143.

McVee, M.B., Brock, C.H., & Glazier, J.A. (Eds.). (2011). *Sociocultural positioning in literacy: Exploring culture, discourse, narrative, and power in diverse educational contexts.* Cresskill, NJ: Hampton Press.

Miller, S.M., & McVee, M.B. (Eds.). (2012). *Multimodal composing: Learning and teaching for the digital world*. New York: Routledge.

Moll, L.C., Amanti, C., Neff, D., & Gonzalez, N. (1992). Funds of knowledge for teaching: Using a qualitative approach to connect homes and classrooms. *Theory into Practice, 31*(2), 132–141.

New London Group. (1996). A pedagogy of multiliteracies: Designing social features. *Harvard Educational Review, 66*(1), 60–92.

New London Group. (2000). A pedagogy of multiliteracies: Designing social futures. In B. Cope & M. Kalantzis (Eds.), *Multiliteracies: Literacy learning and the design of social futures* (pp. 9–37). New York: Routledge.

Nieto, S. (2002). *Language, culture, and teaching: Critical perspectives for a new century*. Mahwah, NJ: Lawrence Erlbaum.

Pahl, K., & Rowsell, J. (Eds.). (2006). *Travel notes from the new literacy studies*. Tonawanda, NY: Multilingual Matters Ltd.

Pearce, S. (2003). Compiling the White inventory: The practice of whiteness in a British primary school. *Cambridge Journal of Education, 33*(2), 273–288.

Phillon, J., He, M.F., & Connelly, F.M. (2005). *Narrative and experience in multicultural education*. Thousand Oaks, CA: Sage.

Raphael, T.E., & McMahon, S.I. (1994). Book club: An alternative framework for reading instruction. *The Reading Teacher, 48*(2), 102–106.

Raphael, T.E., Pardo, L.S., & Highfield, K. (2002). *Book club: A literature-based curriculum* (2nd ed.). Lawrence, MA: Small Planet Communications.

Rist, R.C. (1970). Student social class and teacher expectations: The self-fulfilling prophecy in ghetto education. *Harvard Educational Review, 40*, 411–451.

Rogers, T., Marshall, E., & Tyson, C.A. (2006). Dialogic narratives of literacy, teaching, and schooling: Preparing literacy teachers for diverse settings. *Reading Research Quarterly, 41*(2), 202–224.

Rowsell, J., & Pahl, K. (2007). Sedimented identities in texts: Instances of practice. *Reading Research Quarterly, 42*(3), 388–404. doi:10.1598/RRQ.42.3.3

Santoro, N. (2007). 'Outsiders' and 'others': 'Different' teachers teaching in culturally diverse classrooms. *Teachers and Teaching: Theory and Practice, 13*(1), 81–97.

Santoro, N., Kamler, B., & Reid, J. (2001). Teachers talking difference: Teacher education and the poetics of anti-racism. *Teaching Education, 12*(2), 191–200.

Scribner, A.P., Scribner, J.D., & Reyes, P. (Eds.). (1999). *Lessons from high-performing Hispanic schools*. New York: Teachers College Press.

Shanahan, L.E. (2012). Use of sound with digital text: Moving beyond sound as an add-on or decoration. *Contemporary Issues in Technology and English Language Arts, 12*(3). Retrieved from http://www.citejournal.org/vol12/iss3/languagearts/article1.cfm

Shanahan, L.E., & Roof, L.M. (2013). Developing strategic readers: A multimodal analysis of a primary school teacher's use of speech, gesture, and artefacts. *Literacy, 47*(3), 157–164. doi:10.1111/lit.12002

Snow, C.E., Barnes, W.S., Chandler, J., Goodman, I.F., & Hemphill, L. (1991). *Unfulfilled expectations: Home and school influences on literacy*. Cambridge, MA: Harvard University Press.

Strong-Wilson, T. (2007). Moving horizons: Exploring the role of stories in decolonizing the literacy education of White teachers. *International Education, 37*(1), 114–131.

Tannen, D. (1998). *The argument culture: Stopping America's war of words*. New York: Ballantine Publishing Group.

Timperley, H.S., & Phillips, G. (2003). Changing and sustaining teachers' expectations through professional development in literacy. *Teaching and Teacher Education, 19*(6), 627–641. doi:10.1016/S0742–051X(03)00058–1

Weis, L., Cipollone, K., & Jenkins, H. (2014). *Class warfare: Class, race, and college admissions in top-tier secondary schools.* Chicago: University of Chicago Press.

2

PERSONAL AND CULTURAL NARRATIVES

What We Can Learn and Do Through Story

Have you ever thought your life was ordinary, perhaps even mundane? Have you wondered about people who were not like you and thought that their lives must be exotic and unusual—after all, maybe they spoke a different language or perhaps had different skin tones, hair colors, or facial features from you or your family? Have you ever assumed that "culture" resided somewhere else in someone else—some far-off place where people are dressed in brightly colored clothes like those in National Geographic articles?

Many of us have shared these views of culture as something exotic, something *mis concep* that resides out there in someone else in some other place. Or, perhaps we think of *abt* culture as only that part of our lives saved for celebrating a heritage (i.e., making *culture* spring rolls on Chinese New Year or Irish bread on St. Patrick's Day). But the truth is that all of us are born into and surrounded by cultural communities that shape our perceptions, beliefs, values, attitudes, and desires from the moment we are born. While these cultural communities may not seem exotic, far away, or worthy of a National Geographic moment, they are nonetheless cultural experiences. That is to say, we all have a culture, and more often than not multiple cultures, that shape our ways of interacting with others and even our beliefs about teaching and learning.

In the vignettes below, we, Mary and Fenice, share some of our stories with you. As you read through the narratives below, attend to what *connects* resonates with you or what feels unfamiliar. What cultural practices or beliefs do you see embedded in these stories? What stories might you tell of your earliest cultural communities and the practices within them?

Mary McVee

As someone raised in a remote, rural environment in the northeast corner of the state of Montana in the US, just an hour's drive south of the Canadian border, it always seemed to me that others had a culture. To my childhood imagination even the Canadians were exotic; they had French printed on everything alongside the English! It wasn't until I left my home for university that I began to realize that I resided in a specialized cultural niche, that the ways of talking, thinking, and acting and the cultural values that had governed my childhood were not those shared by others.

I grew up on a cattle ranch in a remote corner of Montana. Standing on the rim of the valley above my home, there is no question about the meaning of Montana's moniker: Big Sky Country. To the east, crested wheat grasses follow the prairie landscape to a barbed wire fence that squares off a field that over the years has contained prairie grass, wheat, or barley. To the north, gently sloping hills give way to coulees that often have a sheer 50-foot drop down into Cherry Creek (always pronounced "crick"). These bottomlands are reminiscent of the Dakota badlands with patches of shale, mica, or isinglass; sagebrush; and drought-resistant grasses. In summer, the cottonwoods form a stretch of green following the mostly dry creek bed south, until, in wet years, the creek emerges in two spring-fed streams that trickle south on both sides of the valley. The two branches of the creek merge into one alongside alfalfa-covered hayfields below a gravelly, glacier-carved hillside.

Northeast Montana is beautiful and rugged—a landscape of extremes. The highest summer temperature recorded was 113 degrees and the lowest −59 (not a wind chill, but actual thermometer reading!). With the biting arctic Canadian wind coming down from the north, dramatic temperature changes are not uncommon. Average annual rainfall is about 12 inches, but in dry years, for example, all throughout my childhood, rainfall was much less. The driest year on record was the year after I graduated from high school when recorded annual rainfall was 6.74 inches. Keeping with the land of extremes, the next summer it rained nearly 5 inches in 24 hours.

As a child I was an avid reader. Although I have three siblings, we lived too far from town and too far from the nearest neighbors to have play dates. Bus rides to and from school were often an hour or more, allowing plenty of time for reading. To the many bumps in the road—what we called "washboards"—my other hobby on the bus seemed to be upchucking my breakfast. Needless to say, reading was the preferred way to spend the time. In thinking back to my own reading (and writing) practices, it is intriguing to me that by third grade I was fascinated by biographies and autobiographies, even memorizing the Dewey Decimal number for biographies on the spine of my books just from seeing it so often. Before I left Irle Elementary School in sixth grade, I had read every biography listed under this number. These books gave me my first glimpses into other lives as I read about famous explorers Daniel Boone and John Colter and American leaders Abraham Lincoln and George Washington, but also less traditional heroes and heroines such as Susan B. Anthony, Elizabeth Blackwell, Frederick Douglass, Harriet Tubman, George Washington Carver, and Clara Barton. These stories reinforced the patriotic images of America I received from my home and community, but this literature also added to my beliefs that the United States was a country where all people could achieve their dreams even in the face of adversity and by challenging injustice. These stories also emphasized the idea that education and learning (e.g., even though Lincoln did not attend college, he studied on his own) were important. My own dream was to go to college. My parents, who had not been able to attend college, encouraged this dream, but were specific in their talk. It would require hard work and scholarships because they could not afford to pay my way; I would need to save money for college. I took their advice literally and started saving for college in first grade, putting any birthday money—usually less than $20—into a savings account each year.

Although I had some rough spots, I managed to do well in high school, received several scholarships, federal Pell grants for low-income students, and worked my way through school while attending the University of Montana, Missoula. The university was the first clear border-crossing experience, where the invisible lines of culture and socioeconomic class differences really became visible to me. I share the following story with students in my language, literacy, and culture class:

> It was 1983, and I was seventeen, a freshman newly arrived to the University of Montana campus. I had grown up in the eastern part of the state on a cattle ranch thirteen miles from the closest small town. For school we were bused one or one-and-a-half hours to school. Twelve years after I began school I graduated with 90 students in my class, most of whom I had known for most of my life, some since I first began riding the bus. Coming to a university of 7,000 students (tiny compared to Michigan State's 40,000+!) was intimidating to me. One of my first experiences was to take a written placement test for freshman composition in one room with several hundred undergraduates. Sitting on tiered platforms in odd-shaped desks, we were given blue books, told to choose from two topics provided, and given a half hour to write. Looking around, I knew no one. No one knew me. And I had never taken a timed writing exam. Although I believed I was a good writer (I'd won several awards, received good grades, and hoped to be a "real author" someday), I failed this test quite miserably and was assigned to a remedial composition class. . . .

Fenice Boyd

I grew up in the "Jim Crow" south in a rural farm community in northeastern North Carolina. Cotton and tobacco fields were rampant throughout the county because these products were the primary way that many families earned their living. Others worked in the textile industry, spinning cotton to make yarn that had been picked from the cotton fields all across the state.

My maternal grandparents were sharecroppers, and my family—grandparents, great uncle, mother, and two brothers—lived in a small wooden house that was about a quarter of a mile off the main road and in the woods. We had a big front and back yard—lots of room for my brothers and I to run and play. My grandmother liked to garden, and she planted all kinds of flowers and greenery. Her landscaping skills ran amuck because anything that she could find to plant in her yard she did.

Our house didn't have indoor plumbing, but rather a well out in the backyard. It was deep—just perfect for yelling down and hearing an echo. Every time we needed water to drink, cook, bathe, or wash laundry, we had to "draw water" from that well, and it took a long time because we could only draw one bucket at a time. There was a small table in the kitchen right beside the stove (we did have electricity) where we always kept two silver buckets of water. One of the chores that my brothers and I had to do was keep those two buckets filled with water, especially when Grandma Davis needed to cook and at night before we went to bed. Eventually the water in the well went dry, and one of our neighbors Miss Winnie and her husband Mr. Archie got running water with a faucet outside, so we would walk to their house to get water. It only took two minutes to run over to Miss Winnie's house to get water, but as a child carrying a bucket of water it felt like I was running a 5K!

My parents separated (and eventually divorced) when my youngest brother, Lawrence, was less than one year old, and my mother—now 87 years old—thinks of herself as a single mother at the same time that she acknowledges the love and support she received from her parents while rearing my two brothers (Wayne and Lawrence) and me. But when I think about my mother as a single parent—I'm also divorced and a single mother of two adult children—while among the poor working class, my mother had it "good!" My brothers and I lived in the house with our grandparents, and when we came home from school, Grandma Davis had a hot dinner on the table; it may have been lima beans with a piece of "fat back" for flavoring and hot biscuits, but it was cooked and ready to eat. When Wayne, Lawrence, and I started first grade, Grandma Davis and Granddaddy were retired sharecroppers, so they were always at home. Grandma Davis was my mother's live-in maid, cook, laundress, counselor, tutor, nurse, and disciplinarian for us. When I think about the differences in our single-parent experiences, my mother had a great deal of support, especially from her mother, but also from our community, and even today, she is not shy about telling people, "Momma raised my children."

While my mother did graduate from high school, she did not go to college. She had an enduring work ethic all of her life, accepting work for what was often less than minimum wage—such as cleaning the homes of affluent Whites, working at a dry cleaners, and eventually working in the textile industry as a factory worker. At the time, pursuing factory work was considered a "good job" because in addition to better pay, being employed at the factory included some benefits.

[handwritten margin note: Why this in us?]

There were also two families who lived within a two-minute walk from our house. Though we were not related to these families biologically, we were family in many ways. In theory, I had "uncles, aunts, and older cousins" within close proximity who provided guidance and support. We were neighbors, but more than neighbors; we were family, but not blood related; we shared resources (borrowing a cup of sugar or a stick of butter), but knew not to take each other for granted as we shared food from gardens during harvest season, and when it was time to slaughter hogs, the meat was shared too. We carpooled when going to Sunday school and to town. When one family drove "up north" to visit relatives, if my mother and grandmother allowed it, I went on the trip too. When it was time for me to start first grade, Miss George Anna gave me my first writing tablet and a "big fat pencil" that young children used to write with at the time.

I attended first through eighth grades at John R. Hawkins School; a campus of various buildings that primarily was founded to prepare "colored" children for manual labor (e.g., mechanics, brick masonry, cooks). Some students were prepared to be leaders, teachers, and preachers, and maybe one or two lawyers or doctors. My classmates and I were taught to take pride in ourselves no matter what profession we chose; we had a very close-knit community. But after eighth grade, I had to leave the school that I had attended all my life. John R. Hawkins School, where I had expected to continue my education, was dismantled and became an elementary school. I was sent to John Graham Senior High School—a school that was predominantly for White students. It was 1969, and fourteen years after *Brown vs. Board of Education*, Warren County North Carolina had decided to fully integrate its schools.

REFLECTION POINT

1. What observations can you make about the stories shared by Mary and Fenice?
2. What differences or similarities might you see across their stories? Between their stories and your own?
3. Why do you think Mary and Fenice chose to start this book with narratives about their experience?
4. What experiences of family, community, language, and culture shaped your early schooling experiences, particularly your experiences with literacy?

The Power of Stories

"Guess what happened today at work?" "Wait 'til you hear this . . ." "Did you hear the story about the guy who . . ." Stories are all around us. They connect

(margin note: Importance of Stories)

us together and entertain us. But, psychologists and anthropologists argue that stories or narratives do more than entertain. Narratives both represent and shape experience. That is, narratives mediate our understanding, construction, and interpretation of life events. When we tell stories, write stories, or compose stories multimodally, for example, through video, collage, a spoken-word poem, or the latest digital communications, we are using narrative structures in ways that not only communicate, but also shape how we position ourselves and others. From this vantage point, stories have tremendous power to help us construct others and ourselves as we wish to be seen or understood, and as we wish others to be seen and understood. We can use this narrative power as a tool to help us explore our beliefs and attitudes about language, literacy, and culture in ways that help us to become better teachers, perhaps even better people. But, at the same time, stories can also reify and isolate. One key element of using narratives in a productive way to is to acknowledge the ways in which narrative can nurture empathy. Rather than using narrative to reify our own positions, beliefs, and identities, we can use narrative to explore what psychologist Jerome Bruner (1990) calls "possible selves," those selves that we might become, hope to become, or even fear we could become (p. 41).

(margin note: note)

Earlier in this chapter you read the narratives we crafted. These narratives reflect selves in the process of becoming. Clearly, we are well past the ages of the narratives of those adolescent or young adult selves where we ended our stories, but how we tell those stories reflects who we feel we have come to be, how we came to be, and even who we might desire to be at a point in the future. In such a perspective the notions of "self" and "identity" are not fixed, but are fluid and active because we are members of multiple and overlapping communities (New London Group, 1996). But, you will also observe that the stories are left open, and there are many possible narrative threads that each story could potentially follow. Stories are not merely written scripts that become static plot lines once shared or written down. This is one of the hallmarks of narrative as used in this text.

Narrative Is Constructive, Dynamic, and Fluid. We Shape and Reshape Ourselves and Our Relationships with Others Through Stories.

In framing these explorations of culture and literacy, we will introduce five hallmarks of narrative. Obviously, there is much more that has been written about narrative than these five hallmarks. You will see examples of narratives throughout this book, and you can read more about narratives and narrative research by consulting the references at the end of this chapter.

It may seem obvious, but we remind our students that any one of us can only begin learning something from where we are. Another way to think of this is that we begin learning from our local vantage point. Many scholars who work with teachers have encouraged educators to understand the local knowledge that children and youth bring into school classrooms. Scholars such as Luis Moll and his colleagues have encouraged teachers to become aware of the "funds of knowledge" (Moll, Armanti, Neff, & Gonzalez, 1992) that children of Mexican descent bring to school from their local Arizona school communities. Hillary Janks (2010), writing about South Africa's diverse contexts, has acknowledged that teachers can help create transformative experiences where they engage children in literate practices that build up and connect local knowledge with global knowledge. While these practices are encouraged for teachers to consider in working with children, seldom have teacher educators documented how they begin building upon localized teacher knowledge with preservice and inservice teachers or other educators. Just as scholars have advocated storytelling as a means for knowledge construction for children and youth in classrooms, so too narrative can be a powerful means of helping teacher educators understand the localized understandings and knowledge that adult learners bring to their adult classroom learning communities. Examining our local knowledge and the positions we take up around that knowledge requires that we attend to self and others. It also requires that we attend closely to the role that language plays in the development of our own identities and our views of others. This brings us to our second hallmark of narrative:

Narratives Can Assist Teachers in Attending to Their Own Local Knowledge and to Their Students' Local Knowledge

Gaining an awareness of our own local knowledge or local knowledge of our students requires listening and attending carefully to the stories we construct along and together. This process of looking at self and asking "Who am I?" and looking toward others "Who are you?" offers the potential to create knowledge about others, and importantly, to explore empathetic response.

The author Azar Nafisi (2003) has written powerfully about the visionary and empathic function of literature in *Reading Lolita in Tehran*. After her dismissal from her university teaching post for refusing to wear the veil, Nafisi organized a clandestine book discussion group. This group provided young women a safe and unconstrained environment for the discussion of literature. The openness of the group's discussions contrasted with the increasingly oppressive Iranian regime and its policies of censorship. As an astute observer, Nafisi argued that tight governmental controls deadened the individual's ability to empathize with others. She contrasted her analysis of the larger social, political, and religious contexts with the literature discussion group where women talked about literature and their own lives, noting: "Other people's sorrows and joys have a way of reminding us of our own; we partly empathize with them because we ask ourselves: What about me? What does this say about my life, my pains . . .?" (p. 325).

In considering Sylvia Scribner's landmark studies of the literacy of the Vai people in Liberia, Florio-Ruane (2002) draws attention to both empathy and local knowledge as she describes a blending of heart and mind in which Scribner "invites the reader to reflect on his or her own folk wisdom and local knowledge by asking, 'What does literacy mean in my life, time, and society? How do my tacitly held norms and values for its practice limit my thinking about other literacies? What responsibilities do I have, as a person empowered to make decisions affecting the literate lives of others ...?'" (p. 213). These are the questions that can be explored through our own stories and the stories of others and are the third hallmark of narrative:

Narratives Can Help Us to Acknowledge and Develop Empathic Stances Toward Others

---

REFLECTION POINT

1. Can you think of a time when a story (through whatever mode it was presented, for example, writing, visual art, music, etc.), helped you to feel an affinity for a certain group?
2. Is there a time when you felt that a story isolated or alienated you in some way?
3. Can you think of a story that challenged your thinking, a story that might have caused you to revisit or attempt to re-story your own narrative?

Often students come to the class we teach in language, literacy, and culture expecting what we call the "three f's"—food, festivals, and fun. To be sure, cultural explorations that involve these "three f's" can be exhilarating. Many of us have experienced summer festivals or markets that play host to numerous special foods, visual cultural trappings, and lots of fun with friends, family, and, often, even complete strangers. Many of us relish this opportunity to learn about other cultures through such festivals and their visual cultural forms such as food and clothing. Often we have been schooled in this metaphor of culture as visual and exotic represented by its physical or material trappings. Such a perspective belies what anthropologists (e.g., Clifford & Marcus, 1986; Said, 1978) refer to as an Orientalist perspective on culture.

An Orientalist perspective on culture represents culture as something situated in others, something exotic and foreign. Sometimes teachers we work with will even say, "I don't have a culture." In fact, all individuals "have" a culture, which means that all individuals experience, live within, or are shaped by and through culture, since culture is not merely comprised of physical artifacts.

To be sure, physical artifacts are part of culture. All of us as humans move through the world in embodied ways. How we hold our bodies, what is acceptable in terms of personal space, body art, clothing, and other physical elements of our embodied selves are clearly related to our cultural selves. But much of what we most identify with in terms of culture has to do with patterns of thinking and interacting. Consider the way that anthropologist Michelle Rosaldo (1984) describes culture:

> [C]ultural patterns—social facts—provide the template for all human action, growth, and understanding. Culture so construed is, furthermore a matter less of artifacts and propositions, rules, schematic programs, or beliefs, than associative chains and images that tell what can be reasonably linked up with what; we come to know it through collective stories that suggest the nature of coherence, probability and sense within the actor's world. (M. Rosaldo, in Bruner, 1986, p. 66)

Stories help us to surface what Rosaldo calls "associative chains and images" to further explore them, identify them, and then perhaps own them or revise them toward our possible selves. From this perspective culture is less about the visual and more about the discursive. That is, it is more about the language that constructs and represents reality as we understand it and about how language and thought are created through enaction—means and ways of engaging in the world. This is the fourth tenant of narrative:

Narratives Help Foster Explorations of Culture as Discursive and Embodied Rather Than Culture as Merely Visual or Exotic

As you look back at the beginning of this chapter you may see in our stories elements of culture as visible, but also elements of culture as discursive. We also urge you to continue your examination of culture through your own stories. One of the ways that you might do this is to construct a narrative vignette of a border-crossing experience.

NARRATIVE VIGNETTE ABOUT A BORDER CROSSING EXPERIENCE[1]

- Think about a time when you, a friend, or family member tried to enter a new social arena, had your beliefs challenged by a new experience, or had a school or other experience that underscored differences between the private world of family/culture/race/gender/class/religious belief/sexual orientation/language use, etc., and the public world of school or other important institutions.

(Continued)

- Your story should be related to "culture" as broadly construed, but need not be directly related to literacy or education. It can be about related social and cultural concerns such as race, mother tongue, ethnicity, class, or geographic location. (Although stories of travel in another country are literally and metaphorically border crossings, we urge readers to choose these only as a last resort as the often fall into portrayals of culture as exotic). Record your vignette in "free writing" to whatever detail and length you desire. We find a single-spaced one-half- to one-page typed page or 200–700 words is a good start. You should write relatively quickly and without excessive concern for editing, revising, or polishing.
- Your aim is to take what otherwise might be an ordinary life event and shape it into a "story worth telling." Mary's final story about going to college was written in response to this activity and can be used as one simple model.
- Over time you can reflect, revisit, and retell this story to uncover new interpretations and dimensions.

One of the things that often comes through in these narrative vignettes are moments of displacement, often profound, but always discomfiting. Brock and her colleagues (2006) observe that "displacement spaces are places we move into (either by force or choice) whereby we see things differently. Thus, displacement spaces offer potentially fertile ground for growth. Of course, pain can also be associated with growth" (p. 38). These moments of displacement can help provide opportunity to explore aspects of culture that make us feel uneasy—whether that discomfort is caused by race, class, gender, sexuality, or cultural norms related to ways of acting, talking, thinking, believing, or valuing.

In our opening vignettes we left off as our stories were at this point, when both Mary and Fenice had entered a new and unknown space. In retrospect, we believe that our respective struggles in college and high school were, as Brock says, "fertile ground for growth." We learned a lot and reframed our stories in some important ways. Concomitantly, those times of growth also involved both risk and pain. There was fear of failure and fear of change. In Fenice's case, there was also the added fear for her physical safety during this turbulent time period. We do not say this to belittle those experiences, but to note that displacement and reflection upon displacement stories can create fertile ground for new growth. Furthermore, we note that while we use these personal stories for illustrative purposes, we do not suggest that Mary's and Fenice's experiences were equal. Obviously, the struggles, fears, and triumphs that Fenice and other African Americans faced in integrating southern schools were much more challenging than the hurdle Mary faced related to her writing exam and placement and crossing socioeconomic boundaries. In sum, the final hallmark of narrative for this chapter is:

Narrative Helps Us Explore, Understand, and Analyze Displacement Spaces in Our Lives

Why Narrative?

Stories are multilayered and multifaceted. We may tell the same story to two different people in two different ways. We may even tell the same story to one person in two or three or more ways! The text that you are currently reading is about stories, but it is about stories as a process. Whether we are reading and discussing autobiographies, ethnographies, or other stories in Book Club or whether we are composing our own stories, the stories are not ends in and of themselves. The stories are necessary but insufficient conditions for learning. To truly learn, we must enter a space with the freedom to recognize that it is the act of narrating, constructing, representing, and examining that is critical. This process helps us to discover, to recognize, and to name the various positions we assign to ourselves and to others, and where we are comfortable doing so, to engage in the hard work of repositioning ourselves.

In so doing, we gain the freedom to recognize what "The whole point of stories is not 'solutions' or 'resolutions' but a broadening and even a heightening of our struggles—with new protagonists and antagonists introduced, with new sources of concern or apprehension or hope, as one's mental life accommodates itself to a series of arrivals: guests who have a way of staying, but not necessarily staying put" (Coles, 1989, p. 129). We invite you to usher in your stories. Sit down with them. Invite the rest of us to come along, but don't prepare to settle in and become comfortable. Instead, take a risk. Prepare to look for the displacement spaces where learning can be exhilarating, tentative, and even a little scary.

Note

1. This activity was adapted from the work of Susan Florio-Ruane.

References

Brock, C., Wallace, J., Herschbach, M., Johnson, C., Raikes, B., Warren, K., . . . & Poulsen, H. (2006). Negotiating displacement spaces: Exploring teachers' stories about learning and diversity. *Curriculum Inquiry, 36*(1), 35–62.

Bruner, J. (1986). *Actual minds, possible worlds.* Cambridge, MA: Harvard University Press.

Bruner, J. (1990). *Acts of meaning.* Cambridge: Harvard University Press.

Clifford, J., & Marcus, G.E. (Eds.). (1986). *Writing culture: The poetics and politics of ethnography.* Berkeley, CA: University of California Press.

Coles, R. (1989). *The call of stories: Teaching and the moral imagination*. Boston: Houghton Mifflin.

Florio-Ruane, S. (2002). More light: An argument for complexity in studies of teaching and teacher education. *Journal of Teacher Education, 53*(3), 205–215.

Janks, H. (2010). *Literacy and power*. New York: Routledge.

Moll, L.C., Armanti, C., Neff, D., Gonzalez, N. (1992). Funds of knowledge for teaching: Using a qualitative approach to connect homes and classrooms. *Theory into Practice, 31*(2), 132–141.

Nafisi, A. (2003). *Reading Lolita in Tehran*. New York: Random House.

New London Group (1996). A pedagogy of multiliteracies: Designing social features. *Harvard Educational Review, 66*(1), 60–92.

Rosaldo, M.Z. (1984). Toward an anthropology of self and feeling. In R.A. Shweder & R.A. LeVine (Eds.), *Culture theory: Essays on mind, self, and emotion* (pp. 137–157). Cambridge: Cambridge University Press.

Said, E.W. (1978). *Orientalism*. New York: Pantheon Books.

3

GETTING THE CONVERSATION STARTED

Principles, Structure, and Organization in Multicultural Book Clubs

with Taffy E. Raphael

REFLECTION QUESTIONS

1. What ideas or images come to mind when you hear the term "book club"?
2. Have you ever participated in a book club? (This could have been as a child, youth, or adult.)
3. What do you recall about your book club?
4. In your work with children, have you facilitated a book club or literature discussion? If so, how did you facilitate the discussion around texts and what did you learn?

What Is a Book Club?

Many of us can likely conjure up an image of a book club discussion even if we have not participated in one. As teachers, we may picture children sitting around a table, fidgeting in their seats as they wait their turn to talk about a story they have read. Or maybe we picture adults around a table with coffee, tea, and refreshments on the table while people question, argue, and comment with a book in hand. This notion of a book club is part of what Raphael and her colleagues portray in their work with Book Club for children and adolescents, and it is also part of what Raphael and Florio-Ruane had in mind when implementing Book Club for adults. But, this image of people talking about a book with one another provides only the barest essential of what a book discussion might be. Book Club, whether for children, adolescents, or adults, requires thoughtful planning, support, and encouragement, as well as a great deal of effort.

In this chapter, we will begin exploring some foundational aspects of book discussion and Book Club as conceptualized by Taffy Raphael and Susan Florio-Ruane and their colleagues. (To assist readers, a representative sample of publications is available at the end of this chapter.) Our end goal is to become better educators through collaboration and discussion of issues related to literacy, language, and culture in order to teach children in ways that enable them to have the needed knowledge, skills, strategies, and dispositions to lead to successful, engaged learning. We thus extend the work that Raphael and Florio-Ruane have begun by exploring the context of adult multicultural book discussions.

What Do You Notice?

Before we talk about the structure of Book Club, let's take a look at a group of four preservice and inservice teachers engaging in a peer-led Book Club. In the following vignette, Book Club members Bridget, Eve, Kathryn, Lillian, and Terry discuss *Always Running: La Vida Loca: Gang Days in LA*, a memoir by Luis Rodriguez (1993). In the book Rodriguez describes his youth in east LA, his involvement in gang life, schooling, his interest in writing, and his emerging identity as a young man. While at times the writing is poetic, it also contains raw descriptions and portraits of gang life and violence. The narrative does not follow a linear, chronological order, but skips backward and forward. This structure can cause confusion for some readers.

Later, we will present an analysis of what we see in this discussion, but first, we want you to consider what you notice here. Read through the following excerpt (or if you are in a group you may want to choose to represent a participant and read through it like a script or a reader's theatre, where everyone takes on one part to read aloud):

Kathryn: What did you think about the book? I did not like it.
Terry: I didn't either because I like stories where I can make some kind of connection . . . and I couldn't. When I was writing this (referring to her Book Log), a lot of it is a series of quotes because I couldn't come up with . . .
Lillian: It's [the book's] symbolic.
Eve: I had a hard time finding themes. Like when I was reading the *Holler [If You Hear Me]* book, they popped out really quickly while I was reading it. But I think that's because it was from the perspective of a teacher, so we more easily identified. But when I was reading this book, I didn't approach it as I'm supposed to learn something as a teacher, more as, in order for me to be an effective teacher. I thought to [Kathy] Au [1988, "Personal narratives, literacy, portfolios, and

culture"] and the way she starts the beginning of her article is that in order to be an effective teacher you need to have an understanding of the culture. So I kinda saw the book as kind a two-fold. One, he was writing this book to give us a background on the gang culture so that if we ever did teach . . . give us a greater idea of what that culture was about, but then also to kind of come to an understanding—like a social understanding—of, we need to understand others in order to be more effective . . .

Kathryn: When I read the book I thought, "Oh my God," and then I looked at the article and I thought, you know, if I would've ever grown up like this, if I would've had parents like this, what would've happened to me? If I would've grown up in a ghetto—I mean, in our house there was never even the discussion if I was ever going to finish high school. That was not a point of discussion. That was not a point of discussion if I would attend college or not and I knew that was just like breakfast, dinner, lunch . . . breakfast, lunch, and dinner. But that was just something that was there. But what would've happened to me if I would've been in their shoes? And then my thing was, would I have had the strength to get out? And I don't think I would have.

**REFLECTION POINT: HOW DO
GROUP MEMBERS RESPOND?**

1.   What do you notice about how Kathryn starts the talk in this Book Club?
2.   Is Kathryn's approach a beneficial way to start a group discussion? Why or why not?
3.   Beyond Kathryn's opening, what else do you notice about the group's interaction?
4.   What do you notice about each member's individual contribution or talk?

Read the analysis below and see how it compares to your thoughts about the transcript. We discuss various group interactions and use them to illustrate a principle of Book Club.

Explorations at the Beginning of a Book Club Discussion

In the excerpt above, Kathryn starts off the evening's discussion with a question that any of us might ask our peers about a book:

Kathryn: What did you think about the book? I did not like it.
Terry: I didn't either because I like stories where I can make some kind of connection . . . and I couldn't. When I was writing this (referring to

her Book Log), a lot of it is a series of quotes because I couldn't come up with . . .

Lillian: It's [the book] symbolic.

Eve: I had a hard time finding themes.

Terry agrees with Kathryn, noting that she (Terry) did not like the book either because she could not relate to it. She acknowledges another important element of her preparation for Book Club, her Book Log, which she indicates is comprised of a series of quotes. Terry doesn't have a chance to explain completely what she "couldn't come up with" because she is interrupted by Lillian who posits that the book is symbolic—another topic that is not immediately picked up. Lillian's comment is followed in rapid succession by Eve who observes she had a difficult time identifying themes in the book.

The discussion does not start off with contrived roles or activities. On this night, Kathryn speaks up with the first question asking what others think about the book. Terry, Lillian, and Eve respond in a conversational manner while Bridget, another group member, listens in. The talk in the group evolves over time with participants taking up some questions, ignoring others, raising themes, referencing the book, characters, setting, or even participants' own lives, and this illustrates our first principle:

Book Club Principle #1: Book Club Is Authentic

In the excerpt, Terry notes that she struggled to connect with Rodriguez's memoir and suggests that this affected her Book Log. Instead of a more personal response, she chose a series of quotes from the book. While this may be seen as a limitation, Terry is aware of wanting a way into the book, a connection, and she raises this topic with the group. Although it is not required, it is not uncommon for students to start off with direct or indirect references to their Book Logs or with sharing. While suggestions are made for how to respond to a book, there are no preset questions for students to answer or prefabricated prompts. This allows Book Club discussions to be authentic, as noted above, but it also allows responses to literature to be constructed, rather than prescribed, and to be open-ended with many options for student choice. This does not mean, however, that there is no support for learners. As we will demonstrate across the following chapters, there are ways to support individual student and group responses to literature through Book Club.

Book Club Principle #2: Book Logs and Responses to Literature Are Chosen and Constructed by the Learner but Supported by the Teacher if Necessary

After comments made by Kathryn, Terry, and Lillian, Eve takes the first extended turn of talk:

Eve: I had a hard time finding themes. Like when I was reading the *Holler [If You Hear Me]* book, they popped out really quickly while I was reading it. But I think that's because it was from the perspective of a teacher, so we more easily identified. But when I was reading this book, I didn't approach it as I'm supposed to learn something as a teacher, more as, in order for me to be an effective teacher. I thought to [Kathy] Au (1998) and the way she starts the beginning of her article ["Personal narratives, literacy, portfolios, and culture"] is that in order to be an effective teacher you need to have an understanding of the culture. So I kinda saw the book as kind a two-fold. One, he was writing this book to give us a background on the gang culture so that if we ever did teach . . . give us a greater idea of what that culture was about, but then also to kind of come to an understanding—like a social understanding—of, we need to understand others in order to be more effective . . .

Here Eve uses her extended turn to engage in several different strategies. First, she compares the current text *Always Running* to a previous text her group had discussed, *Holler If You Hear Me.* She observes her own response: As a teacher she finds she can readily connect with Michie and his students in *Holler,* but she struggles to connect with Rodriguez. But also notice, she does not dismiss Rodriguez immediately, she has clearly considered: "Why am I reading this book?" and "What can I learn from this story?" In so doing, she identifies an important issue that her group could take up for discussion as they engage in a critical analysis and infer various purposes for their reading. Eve also makes an important intertextual connection; she positions her own life text (that of a teacher) next to Rodriguez (a text she feels unconnected to) with Au (a text that connects personal narrative and culture).

Book Club Principle #3: Book Club Affords Opportunities for Analytic Reflection and Intertextual Connections

Eve starts to explore the intertextual connections she introduces, but Kathryn interrupts her elaboration. (In later chapters we will discuss how interruption, interjection, or overlapping talk can be a hindrance or an indication of coherence in discussions, see Chapter 6).

Kathryn: When I read the book I thought, "Oh my God," and then I looked at the article and I thought, you know, if I would've ever grown up like this, if I would've had parents like this, what would've happened to me? If I would've grown up in a ghetto—I mean, in our house there was never even the discussion if I was ever going to finish high school. That was not a point of discussion. That was not a point of discussion if I would attend college or not and I knew that was just like breakfast, dinner, lunch . . . breakfast, lunch and dinner. But that was just something that was there. But what would've happened to me if I would've been in their shoes? And then my thing was, would I have had the strength to get out? And I don't think I would have.

Our purpose in this text is specifically to consider discussions and explorations related to multicultural literature. This includes teacher ethnography, autobiography, journalistic narrative, and research narratives. Kathryn's admission to her group very early on in this discussion indicates the beginning of an empathic response for the character and the challenges he faced in an urban environment with limited economic opportunities. Kathryn was born and raised in Germany but emigrated to the US in her early twenties where she had married and was raising her children. Kathryn's "What if . . ." comments juxtapose her life—one that had been filled with a variety of choices about where to live and which educational opportunities to follow—with the limited choices that often faced Rodriguez. In stepping into Rodriguez's shoes, Kathryn positions herself in the place of the other. This stance holds forth the potential for Kathryn and her group to build empathy with Rodriguez and for Kathryn to explore issues about her own identity and the identities of other cultural and ethnic groups.

Book Club Principle #4: In Addition to Examining Traditional Literary Elements (e.g., Characters, Authors, Events, etc.), a Multicultural Book Club Requires Consideration of One's Own Position.

Sociocultural Positioning Around Language, Literacy, and Culture

This last principle is perhaps most closely tied to the heart of narrative explorations of language, literacy, and culture as discussed in one. Scholars of narrative have long conveyed that we humans use stories not only to represent meaning, but to construct our identities. As we narrate our own stories or explore the stories of others, our talk reveals how we position others and ourselves. In our best moments, our interactions through talk or writing or other modes may cause us to step back, eyes wide open in surprise, as we stumble onto some new recognition of ourselves, whether that be a positive realization or a realization that challenges our current conception of our self-identity.

Given the increasing cultural, linguistic, and ethnic diversity within many countries, it is critical for teachers to consider how culture, language, and ethnic identities shape literacy and language use. Many times when we, as educators, consider these issues, we direct our attention outward, toward children or communities. Often times, external pressures such as testing and standards orient our focus toward identifying the best pedagogical practices for effective teaching leading to increased student achievement. It is important to consider the children, their families, and their communities and to try to understand literate development within such communities. It is critical that these children receive pedagogy that demonstrates effective practice that leads to demonstrated growth and progress in reading and writing. However, unless we first begin by examining ourselves, we run the risk of creating pity instead of empathy, condescension instead of respect, and emotionless efficiency instead of embodied engagement.

Meaningful discussion of various forms of multicultural literature read and explored in combination with our own personal narratives holds forth the potential to open up pathways for communication, to help us explore important, but often contested, terrain that can be difficult to traverse. We argue that Book Club is not only helpful in this regard, but essential. It provides a solid theoretical grounding and useful framework to help foster discussions for preservice and inservice teachers and other educators.

Book Club Structure and Organization

Four Components of Book Club

Within our adult Book Clubs, there are four components adapted from Raphael and her colleagues:

1. Whole-Class Community Share
2. Reading
3. Multimodal Composing
4. Peer-Led Book Clubs

Whole-Class Community Share is an opportunity to share initial responses to a text, raise questions, share Book Logs, and introduce ideas. It is also a time when teachers, whether they are working with children or adults, can introduce supports, scaffolds, strategies, and ideas that may be helpful for individual learners or for further consideration in discussion groups either before or after interacting with texts.

Reading—Given that adult students are proficient readers, most reading is done outside the classroom. We have found two fundamental concepts useful in defining the parameters of what our adult students read. First, we include short readings that students mark up and discuss on the spot in class. This allows instructors to provide guidance around interpretation. Second, and critically important in today's world, our and their expanded definition of reading should include a range of multimodal media (e.g., artwork of all kinds, TED talks, YouTube clips, Animoto productions, commercials, websites, etc.). "Reading" these various types of media in class not only assists preservice and inservice teachers in exploring through multimodal means, but it provides a model for how different media forms, including artwork, can be integrated in the classroom.

[margin annotation: multimodal in classrooms]

Multimodal Composing—Composition (whether digital or traditional) continues to play an important role in adult Book Clubs. Most writing is composed in the Book Club members' Book Logs. However, current and emerging digital technologies allow Book Logs to draw from many forms of expression (see below). While most writing and longer composing is done outside class, in-class writing can be a way for teachers to quickly assess the feelings, thoughts, ideas, and observations of adult Book Club participants.

Peer-Led Book Clubs—These are usually comprised of four to six participants who have read a common piece of literature and who have begun to explore and express some of their ideas about that literary work through their Book Logs. The participants moderate peer-led Book Clubs. There are no assigned roles or prefabricated questions assigned for discussion.

Book Logs

Traditionally Book Club Logs are informal responses (traditionally constructed through writing or drawing for younger children) where Book Club participants construct responses to a book they have read. Book Logs also serve to prepare the reader by providing a means to interact with the text to ask questions, explore content or characters, make inferences, map out positions, and engage in many other activities. Our work with adult Book Clubs and our content focus have led us to adapt the model implemented by Raphael and McMahon. We recommend Book Logs comprised of at least two types of open responses, since adults are capable of thinking and writing in ways different from children and adolescents.

We suggest to our students that they construct their Book Club Log to include one **free-writing section** using linguistic text. Most students are comfortable responding to literature through writing. The free-writing section of the Book Log is a space where Book Club participants can entertain big ideas, themes, and issues. That is, they respond to the text they have read (or multiple texts) in a substantive way. They strive to move beyond a superficial treatment of the text such as summarizing. Students are often very creative in how they engage with the text. They write letters in the voice of a character or write letters to a character. They write poetry or sometimes just respond to get their emotions out. There are many means of responding through writing that Raphael and her colleagues recommend for use with children. Adults who participate in Book Club can use many of these same techniques.

We also recommend that our students include **multimodal responses**. Recent work on multimodality and new literacies has drawn attention to how learners can now layer modes such as image, sound, color, text, movement, etc., in far more complex ways than we could previously (Miller & McVee, 2012). While some students are fairly familiar with these forms of responses, others find this type of response to be challenging. Frequently, our students will use traditional writing to reflect upon and explain their thinking, as well as to explain their multimodal compositions. As their instructors, we appreciate their explanations, which give us greater access to our students' internal reflections and learning. It also provides insights into their close reading of texts.

Examples of a multimodal response could be a movie burned onto DVD, posted on YouTube, or constructed in Animoto. Many students enjoy making digital posters using Glogster or Voice Thread (or a traditional poster on poster board!) or whatever app or tool is in vogue. Over the years, we have had students make sculptures, draw maps, create digital poetry, record interviews, and make altered books electronically or on paper. In requesting a multimodal response, we tap into the power of multimodal literacies and the principle that learning is not just locked into traditional print-based literacies, but is embodied in our identities and the various modes we use for communication.

In this chapter, we have presented the core components of Book Club for students and teachers, with adaptations to reflect 21st-century literacies and related tools and strategies important to our teachers and their students' success. The adaptation to include multimodal response is significant in its implications for teachers' knowledge needed to be successful in creating a Book Club format for classroom discussions. Chapter 4 is devoted to explorations of multimodality and the ways that students and teachers can move beyond print-based composing.

References

Au, K. (1998). Personal narratives, literacy portfolios, and cultural identity. *National Forum of Teacher Education Journal, 8*(1).

Miller, S.M., & McVee, M.B. (Eds.). (2012). *Multimodal composing: Learning and teaching for the digital world*. New York: Routledge.

Rodriguez, L. (1993). *Always running:* La vida loca: *Gang days in LA*. Willimantic, CT: Curbstone Press.

For Further Reading

Book Club with Adults

Florio-Ruane, S. (2001). *Teacher education and the cultural imagination*. Mahwah, NJ: Lawrence Erlbaum.

McVee, M.B., Brock, C.H., & Glazier, J.A. (Eds.). (2011). *Sociocultural positioning in literacy: Exploring culture, discourse, narrative, and power in diverse educational contexts*. Cresskill, NJ: Hampton Press. (See Part II).

Book Club with Children and Youth

Raphael, T.E., Florio-Ruane, S., George, M., Hasty, N.L., & Highfield, K. (2004). *Book club plus! A literacy framework for the primary grades*. Lawrence, MA: Small Planet Communications.

Raphael, T.E., Kehus, M., & Damphousse, K. (2001). *Book club for middle school*. Lawrence, MA: Small Planet Communications.

Raphael, T.E., & McMahon, S.I. (1994). Book club: An alternative framework for reading instruction. *The Reading Teacher, 48*(2), 102–106.

Raphael, T.E., Pardo, L.S., & Highfield, K. (2002). *Book club: A Literature-based curriculum* (2nd ed.). Lawrence, MA: Small Planet Communications.

4

MORE THAN JUST TALK

Multimodal Composing and Embodiment in Explorations of Culture and Identity

with James R. Gavelek and Lisa Roof

In Chapters 2 and 3, we explored how personal narrative and Book Club discussions can assist learners in exploring complex issues related to diversity, literacy, and culture. In this chapter we will consider various perspectives on multimodal composition and how students of all ages can use sound, image, words, movement, and other modes to compose text. These multiple modalities provide additional avenues of meaning making to help learners explore diversity, culture, and literacy in complex ways. For teachers and other educational professionals, approaches to multimodality provide the opportunity to engage in a composition process that they could also, ultimately, use in the classroom with their own students.

REFLECTION QUESTIONS

1. Which of these literacy skills (reading, writing, listening, speaking) are used most by students in schools in the pre-K/primary grades? Upper elementary? Middle school? High school? College?
2. How different is schooling from 10 years ago? 20 years? 50 years?
3. How might current educational and technological trends change the types of literacy skills needed in schools and in learning?
4. How are colors and shapes used to represent or suggest meaning in societies and cultures? Can you think of specific examples?

What Is Multimodal Representation?

Consider the octagon below. What does this octagon mean or represent?

Not sure? Imagine adding some red color. Can you read it now? (Color images, artifacts, and links can be found at marymcvee.com.)

Still not sure? What if we add writing?

Chances are that if we showed you an octagon and asked, "What is this?" You might guess, "Stop sign." If we told you it was a type of sign before asking, you would almost surely guess what it was with some confidence. And, if we added red to the octagonal shape, you would be even more certain. By the time we add the word "stop," whether in Arabic, Chinese, Thai, or English, it seems almost gratuitous! Stop signs, in particular, are so ubiquitous (even around the world, they are often a common shape and color) that the printed letters and words are not the primary carriers of meaning. Instead the meaning is heavily dependent upon shape (an octagon) and color (red and white). These elements of shape and color can be referred to as **modes**. Modes also include print text such as the alphabetic

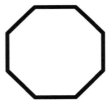

FIGURE 4.1 Black-line octagon.

FIGURE 4.2 Imagine that the octagon is shaded red.

FIGURE 4.3 Arabic, Chinese, Thai, and English stop signs.

scripts for English, Thai, or Arabic or logographic writing systems such as Chinese characters. However, modes go far beyond print or visual elements. Sounds, textures, movement, and spatiality can all be modes that represent meanings. Combining or layering modes together results in a **multimodal** representation. Different modes provide different opportunities or affordances for communicating and creating meaning (Kress, 2009).

The Verbocentric Nature of Formal Schooling

What is interesting is that while we spend most of our lives learning through multiple modes, when we enter formalized schooling, the modalities allowed for taking in information and processing and creating information are often limited. Preschoolers are often encouraged to move, jump, sing, touch, and use vibrant colors while learning. But as children move up the grade levels, there is a shift away from a combined use of these various modes toward a reliance of learning through only a few modes. Formal school learning is heavily dependent upon the linguistic modes of reading and writing or what are sometimes called **verbocentric** practices. Speaking is also important, although many decades of classroom research have shown that oral language use is dominated by teachers (e.g., Mehan, 1979; Cazden, 1988/2001). Students are much less frequently asked to use oral language to construct meaning or explore authentic questions than to recite information that teachers have in mind.

The verbocentric nature of school learning is reflected in many ways (Siegel, 1995). For example, as children learn to read, their ability to do well in school depends, in turn, on their ability to decode text and then to comprehend complex texts. As learners advance, their proficiency with multiple types of texts (e.g., informational, narrative, persuasive) often determines how much success they achieve in school. Educators and researchers alike are familiar with the "fourth grade slump," where students who may have been holding their own in reading or struggling slightly can experience a drop in test scores and performance (Chall & Jacobs, 2003). Even students who have seemed secure in their skills may experience this slump upon encountering more complex informational texts traditionally introduced in fourth grade content areas. And, this verbocentrism is not limited to reading. Writing linguistic text is also important in early school experiences and across the grade levels. Consider, for example, that formal schooling has often emphasized spelling words correctly in written form, writing complete sentences, and ultimately, writing longer formal essays, thus placing an emphasis on a particular product as opposed to constructing knowledge through writing. This narrow approach is also reflected in the ways in which oral discourse is typically used in classrooms. Teachers also often use oral directives to provide instructions, redirect behavior, or explain content directly.

Now, you may be asking yourself: Aren't decoding text, writing complete sentences, and the like required for traditional reading and writing? Isn't it effective to give verbal instructions and deliver content information through the spoken word? And the answer is: Yes, of course, decoding texts and writing words and sentences are essential skills. Oral instructions or directions are sometimes the most efficient and most effective means of delivering information. Also, oral discourse and, in particular, dialogic discussions as noted in Chapter 5 can be valuable learning tools. Rich studies of classroom practice demonstrate that teachers can and do play an important role in fostering learning through complex explorations of text and content through various forms of oral discourse (e.g., Boyd & Galda, 2011, Juzwik, Nystrand, Kelly, & Sherry, 2008). The point we are making here is that formal schooling is typically **verbocentric**, and in most cases it is printcentric. **Printcentric** describes the high status accorded to print through both reading and writing. Traditionally, reading and writing have been *the* primary means of communicating and constructing knowledge in formalized schooling.

While other modes may be used in conjunction with speech or print, verbocentric means of communication dominate formal schooling. We acknowledge that there are some nonlinguistic means of communication that are very common in schools. Two everyday examples are the classic gesture of having students raise their hands to indicate they are willing to answer a question and the action of teachers flicking the lights off and on to indicate that students should settle down and be quiet. Both of these can be effective and efficient management techniques if used thoughtfully. Also, teachers do integrate various modes into teaching using maps, images, music, gesture, and other means. Yet, these representations are still often rather limited in scope; typically these modes are supplemental rather than essential to the meaning being created. Although there are exceptions (see Shanahan & Roof, 2013), teachers often do not focus strategically on delivering content through a particular mode. More importantly, when it comes time for students to process or represent their knowledge, students are asked to complete reading and writing exercises across the content areas, and reading and writing are also used as primary tools in assessing student achievement. In sum, multimodal representations of student knowledge occur far less frequently than traditional reading and writing and often as a supplement or special project.

improvement needed

Multimodality, Social Semiotics, and Embodied Cognition

Many children's books are multimodal—think of the classic *Pat the Bunny* (Kunhardt, 1940) or peekaboo board books, pop-up books, and colorful picture books. Scholars have also found that there has been a shift over the past few decades in academic books for learners of all ages. As printing options have become more complex and color has become less expensive, authors and publishers have included more modalities related to color, image, and font styles. The use of these modalities has shifted from being primarily supplemental toward carrying important information that readers are meant to decode (e.g., see Kress, 2010). Kress observes:

the study of *modes* in multimodal social semiotics focuses on the *material*, the *specific*, the making of signs *now*, in this environment for this occasion. In its focus on the material it also focuses on the bodilyness of those who make and remake signs in constant semiotic (inter)action. It represents a move away from high abstraction to the specific, the material; from mentalistic to the bodily. (p. 13, italics in the original)

What Kress is saying here is that in focusing on modes (e.g., color, font, gesture, animation, and so on), we can examine these as particular signs or ways of making meaning. These signs are socially interpreted and grounded. The stop sign example at the beginning of this chapter functions as both a literal "sign post" that can be put up on a street in our community and as a "sign" representing or communicating meaning. The meaning is both socially and historically situated and created. The red stop sign is a material artifact, but it can also function as a more abstract representation of meaning or even as a symbol.

The first stop sign was reportedly installed in the US city of Detroit, Michigan, in 1915. It had green letters on a white background. Later, stop signs were standardized with the octagonal shape and black letters on a yellow background, and eventually stop signs became red with white reflective STOP (Greenbaum & Rubinstein, 2011). In the US, the color red has become associated with "caution" or "danger" and is used to represent danger in many different ways. Red can also represent love; Valentine's hearts are red, not black or yellow. Red in other cultures has different or additional meanings. For example, in China red means "happiness" and traditionally wedding clothes, festival lanterns, and holiday firecrackers are red. However, no one in China would suggest that a stop sign represents "happiness" because it is red. Multimodal representations are thus, socially, culturally, and historically situated in particular contexts.

But what of the words "bodilyness" and "mentalistic" used by Kress in the quote above? Consider how a teacher might introduce students to a close reading of a poem by parsing the text line by line. The teacher could explain the grammatical and rhythmic construction of the poem, rereading each line multiple times. The teacher might even involve students in reading and rereading lines and ask the class to interpret individual lines to elicit the "correct" interpretation of the poem—"correct" here referring to what the teacher feels is the proper textual interpretation. Alternatively, consider a poem interpreted and represented by a student who uses the multiple modes of images, words, colors, sound, and animations to create a multimodal ensemble that presents her interpretation of the poem. As the student works to create this multimodal poetry interpretation, she must read and reread the poem, attempting to understand its literal meaning and its poetic or metaphoric meaning. As the student works through the design and redesign process, she moves recursively between her newly designed poetry interpretation and the original text, reading, rereading, revising, and clarifying her final design. As she works on her digital interpretation a fellow classmate works on his interpretation of another poem, preparing the text to present it as spoken word poetry combined with his own rap lyrics and print photographs of his neighborhood.

In the first example in the preceding paragraph—the line-by-line parsing of grammar and search for correct meaning—the poem becomes an abstraction—mere words on the page. The teacher analyzes technical aspects and students must "use their heads" (i.e., their mental thought processes) to analyze the poem's technical aspects (or guess how the teacher is analyzing these aspects and interpreting the poem). The latter examples of multimodal poetry interpretations (digital multimodal interpretation or a performed spoken word poem with images) offer opportunities to step away from "in-the-head" abstractions, or what Kress refers to as "mentalistic" models of representation. Involving multiple modes for representation allows a broader swath of bodily representations (e.g., color, sound, movement) and the like. Such performances may even involve the body itself, as in the case of the young man who uses his embodied self to perform a poem using voice, gesture, stance, and image. Embodied approaches emphasize teaching and learning that move away from traditional cognitive, in-the-head-only models of literacy teaching and learning (see McVee, Dunsmore, & Gavelek, 2005; McVee, Gavelek, & Dunsmore, 2007).

A focus on multimodality draws our attention to the modes or the material aspects of signs. And, as noted above, much learning is multimodal. Even *in utero* babies turn toward light or toward their mother's voice. Whereas multimodality stresses the perception and interpretation of the material of mode (e.g., seeing the light or hearing a mother's voice), embodied cognition emphasizes to even greater degree the perceiving of, acting on, and experiencing of various modes of meaning. In literacy, the advent of electronic books has meant that books can easily and cheaply include multiple modes. Color, image, font styles, and the like can be readily included, but electronic books can also include sound, interaction through touch screens, and even responses from the reader. New technologies offer opportunity for the reader to change the story merely by shaking a digital device to change the storyline (see artist Raghava KK's TED Talk: "Shake Up Your Story: http://www.ted.com/talks/raghava_kk_shake_up_your_story.html). Video games are also increasingly sophisticated interactive spaces that are becoming more multimodal through whole body movement and through MMOGs (massively multiplayer online games), where players make choices that shape the game's storyline.

Not only are today's children and youth used to consuming these types of texts, children and youth participate in creating digital texts with ease, navigating through changes in technology and shared social spaces. While attention to multimodal design in educational settings has lagged behind the world of digital and popular media, recent years have seen a burgeoning interest in these issues for teachers, teacher educators, and scholars. However, we still have a long way to go. All teachers can learn a great deal alongside their students and, particularly, *from* their students who often know much more about multimodal design. But, as adult learners, we can also stretch our own understandings of multimodality and [include in text] multimodal design in professional development or teacher education programs focused on adult learning.

It is critical that we experience, enact, and deeply internalize these new understandings in order to avoid giving our teaching a digital makeover on the outside without considering conceptual principles. The shift that we desire educators to undertake is one that influences external behavior and practice, but also influences [ed bias] fundamental beliefs related to education and what it means to learn. Another way of saying this is to note that teachers should learn not only about multimodality, culture, design, or redesign, but teachers must become reflective practitioners (Schön, 1983). Teachers should develop *adaptive expertise* around their pedagogical practice (Darling-Hammond & Bransford, 2005). Adaptive expertise means that teachers learn to reflect but also to adapt pedagogical practices to meet the dynamic needs of learners and teaching (Hayden, Rundell, & Smyntek-Gworek, 2013). In this text, the particular focus on learning is related to understanding **multimodal design** and **social semiotics** as they pertain to explorations of diversity and, ultimately, helping teachers develop knowledge to work with students of all backgrounds.

We conclude this chapter by introducing some multimodal compositions from the work of adult students who were inservice or preservice teachers. We want to again emphasize that while some of these projects were composed using digital technologies, multimodality need not be digital (Albers, 2006). Think of our early ancestors acting out stories in the flickering firelight of a cave, the smell of wood smoke drifting across those seated around the fire, and masked figures acting out a victorious hunt accompanied by rhythmic instruments and voices. Only recently have we acquired digital devices that rapidly and easily allow us to layer multiple modes in new and exciting ways, but humankind has always experienced the world multimodally through our embodied selves. And, as demonstrated by the cave paintings of Zimbabwe, France, or Spain, the pottery of the American Indian pueblos of the Southwest, the glories of Angkor Wat and many other temples, and the long-lived musical traditions of any cultural group of any time period, humankind has a very long history of experimenting with representing meaning through multiple modes. Below you will find examples of student compositions that will help ground our discussion of multimodality in material artifacts and representations.

Multimodal Compositions: Exploring the Affordances of Modes in Design and Explorations of Identity, Culture, Literacy, and Diversity

Student Example 1: Shadowbox

Consider Figure 4.4. This is a shadow box representing themes and insights gained from Greg Michie's (2009) narrative of his years as a novice teacher in an urban school in Chicago. The shadow box is constructed from a shoebox. A city

FIGURE 4.4 Shadow box representing interpretations of *Holler If You Hear Me* (Michie, 2009). (View in color at marymcvee.com.)

scene of high-rise buildings silhouetted against a red sky fills the back of the box. Against this backdrop are many quotes representing the book—its various characters, themes, and ideas. To layer these ideas, the student suspended various quotes and images with pieces of yarn.

Thinking about how different modes afford different meanings, consider these questions:

1. What modes seem to be present in this shadow box?
2. How would the different modes function? That is, how do these various modes help to communicate or represent meanings?
3. What are the affordances that different modes bring?
4. What are the limitations of the various modes and what they afford?
5. What are the benefits and challenges of letting students choose which knowledge they will represent multimodally?
6. Why might it be important to also have additional explanation from students about their work using linguistic text (e.g., speaking or writing about their multimodal project)?

Student Example 2: Digital Video

View "Tribute to the Little Rock Nine," inspired by the book *Warriors Don't Cry* (Beals, 1994) http://www.youtube.com/watch?v=p4XUBGOUdHQ

1. What modes does this student use to craft her tribute?
2. How effective is her representation?
3. Considering "text" in its broadest meaning, what types of informational texts did the student need to explore to construct this video?
4. What types of narrative texts did she need to explore to construct this video?
5. What is your reading and interpretation of this multimodal composition?
6. What social, cultural, and historical information could someone acquire from viewing or "reading" this video?
7. How does this video pertain to themes of social justice, culture, identity, and literacy?

Student Example 3: Digital Poetry Interpretation

View Laura's interpretation of the "Noiseless Patient Spider." Note that you will hear sound in the beginning; the sound will disappear, but then reappear later in the presentation.

http://multimodalpoetry.org/spiderman/LauraSpiderFinal.html

1. What modes does Laura use within this poetry interpretation?
2. How do these modes work together to layer meaning or create rich meanings?
3. In particular, what role do movement and sound play in this composition?
4. What themes does Laura explore in her multimodal composition?
5. What metaphors does she explore? What do these metaphors represent or mean?
6. How does she weave exploration of her own identity into this composition?

Student Example 4: Altered Book

Laura also created an altered book project. For this she used an actual published book that she then altered by adding text, image, various media, objects, and so on to explore themes related to self-identity, race, socioeconomic class, and other diversities. (To view artifacts and color images go to marymcvee.com.)

Did she seek copyright permission?

Laura chooses the metaphor of "knots" to frame her beginning ideas. Why do you think she chose this metaphor? Given your own experiences or explorations of race, identity, and culture, what do you think of this metaphor?

1. How does Laura position herself through this altered book project? How does she position others? What do you feel she is learning?
2. What connections might you draw to insights that other writers (e.g., Adichie, 2009; Florio-Ruane, 1997) have made in analyzing their experiences with understanding identity, culture, narrative, and position?

Student Example 5: Body Biography

A body biography is a visual and written portrait illustrating several aspects of a character's life within a story. The result is a multimodal artifact and is a way for

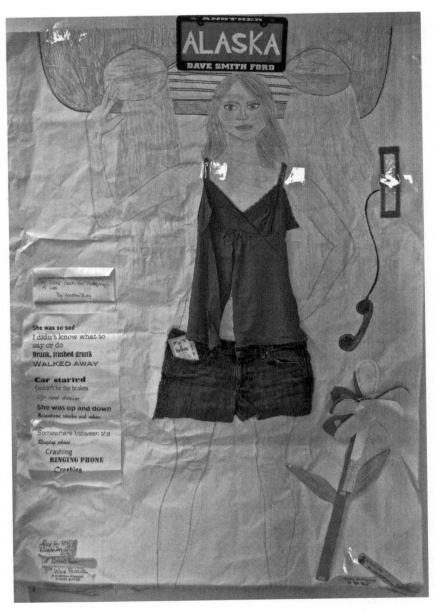

FIGURE 4.5 Body biography representing interpretations of the character Alaska from the young adult novel *Looking for Alaska* (Green, 2005).

students to conduct an in-depth character analysis in lieu of the typical written book report. Students work in small groups (e. g., three to five people) to design their body biography. One major requirement for this project is that students have a responsibility to be creative, analytical, and accurate about the character they choose to represent through a body biography. A second major requirement is that—as a group—students must write a reflective essay that describes the choices selected and the reasons for those choices. In this example, Eleanor, Rylee, Amelia, and Grace designed their body biography to represent Alaska from John Green's novel titled *Looking for Alaska* (2005), a story about the friendship of three teenage friends: Miles, also known as "Pudge," and his roommate Chip and the beautiful but self-destructive Alaska Young who introduces Miles to pranks and adventures but also a search for answers about life.

1.   What modes seem to be present in this body biography?
2.   What artifacts do you see represented in the body biography?
3.   What do these artifacts suggest about Alaska or her story?
4.   How do Eleanor, Rylee, Amelia, and Grace, the students who constructed this biography, use a variety of modes (e.g., linguistic, image, color/shading)?
5.   What might the different modes suggest about Alaska as a main character?

Conclusion

In this chapter we have considered some very basic elements of multimodal design and the affordances of modes. Modes can be powerful tools for exploring and learning about others and ourselves. Modes can also be powerful means of expression and means of idea construction. Bringing multiple modalities together with Book Club and the discussion of complex texts makes for rich opportunities to engage in dialogic interactions around literature.

References

Adichie, C.N. (2009, July). The danger of a single story. [Video File]. Retrieved from http://www.ted.com/talks/chimamanda_adichie_the_danger_of_a_single_story

Albers, P. (2006). Imagining the possibilities in multimodal curriculum design. *English Education, 38*(2), 75–101.

Beals, M. (1994). *Warriors don't cry*. New York: Pocket Books.

Boyd, M.P., & Galda, L. (2011). *Real talk in elementary classrooms: Effective oral language practice*. New York: Guilford Press.

Cazden, C. (1988/2001). *Classroom discourse: The language of teaching and learning*. Portsmouth: Heinemann.

Chall, J.S., & Jacobs, V.A. (2003). Poor children's fourth-grade slump. *American Educator, Spring*. Retrieved from http://www.aft.org/pubs-reports/american_educator/spring2003/chall.html

Darling-Hammond, L., & Bransford, J. (Eds.). (2005). *Preparing teachers for a changing world: What teachers should learn and be able to do*. San Francisco, CA: Jossey-Bass.

Florio-Ruane, S. (1997). To tell a new story: Reinventing narratives of culture, identity, and education. *Anthropology & Education Quarterly, 28*(2), 152–162.

Green, J. (2005). *Looking for Alaska.* New York: Penguin Group.

Greenbaum, H., & Rubinstein, D. (2011, December 9). The stop sign wasn't always red. *The New York Times.* Retrieved from http://www.nytimes.com/2011/12/11/magazine/stop-sign.html

Hayden, H.E., Rundell, T.D., & Smyntek-Gworek, S. (2013). Adaptive expertise: A view from the top and the ascent. *Teaching Education.* doi:10.1080/10476210.2012.724054

Juzwik, M.M., Nystrand, M., Kelly, S., & Sherry, M.B. (2008). Oral narrative genres as dialogic resources for classroom literature study: A contextualized case study of conversational narrative discussion. *American Educational Research Journal, 45*(4), 1111–1154.

Kress, G. (2009). What is mode? In C. Jewitt (Ed.), *The Routledge handbook of multimodal analysis* (pp. 54–67). London: Routledge.

Kress, G. (2010). *Multimodality: A social semiotic approach to contemporary communication.* New York: Routledge.

Kunhardt, D. (1940). *Pat the bunny.* New York: Golden Books.

McVee, M.B., Dunsmore, K.L., & Gavelek, J.R. (2005). Schema theory revisited. *Review of Educational Research, 75*(4), 531–566.

McVee, M.B., Gavelek, J.R., & Dunsmore, K.L. (2007). Considerations of the social, individual, and embodied: A response to comments on "Schema Theory Revisited." *Review of Educational Research, 77*(2), 245–248. doi:10.3102/ 003465430301677

Mehan, H. (1979). "What time is it Denise?" Asking known information questions in classroom discourse. *Theory into Practice, 18*(4), 285–294. doi:10.1080/00405847909542846

Michie, G. (2009). *Holler if you hear me* (2nd ed.). New York: Teachers College Press.

Schön, D.A. (1983). *The reflective practitioner: How professionals think in action.* New York: Basic Books.

Shanahan, L.E., & Roof, L.M. (2013). Developing strategic readers: A multimodal analysis of a primary school teacher's use of speech, gesture and artefacts. *Literacy, 47*(3), 157–164. doi:10.1111/lit.12002

Siegel, M. (1995). More than words: The generative power of transmediation for learning. *Canadian Journal of Education, 20*(4), 455–475.

For Further Reading

McVee, M.B., Bailey, N.M., & Shanahan, L.E. (2008). Using digital media to interpret poetry: Spiderman meets Walt Whitman. *Research in the Teaching of English, 43*(2), 112–143.

Miller, S.M., & McVee, M.B. (Eds.). (2012). *Multimodal composing: Learning and teaching for the digital world.* New York: Routledge.

Pahl, K., & Rowsell, J. (2010). *Artifactual literacies: Every object tells a story.* New York: Teachers College Press.

Serafini, F. (2014). *Reading the visual.* New York: Teachers College Press.

5

TALK THAT WORKS

Moving Toward Engaged Dialogue

[handwritten: Identity Paper on freedom of speech]

REFLECTION QUESTIONS

1. What does dialogue mean to you?
2. What do you think are the hallmarks of a meaningful dialogue?

In Search of Dialogue

In Chapter 4, we explored how crucial aspects of meaning, communication, and representation occur through multiple modes (e.g., color, image, printed words, etc.). Also, we foregrounded multimodality, but we acknowledged that talk (one of the modes that often dominates formal schooling) is important. In this chapter we take a closer look at talk and dialogue.

Although there are yet a few quiet corners of the world, most of us live under a constant barrage of talk—talk news, talk radio, Internet chatter, tweeting, texting, blogging, and so on. With the advent of new technologies, we can talk everywhere and access talk at any time and almost any place. But, how much do we engage in **dialogic talk**? Dialogic talk is talk that requires participants to engage actively in speaking, thinking, *and* listening. In this chapter we will explore what dialogue is and how dialogue can function in Book Club discussions.

What Is Dialogue?

Dialogue is not mere argumentation. This is an especially relevant point given the world we live in where local, national, and global media profit from polarized debates and sensational claims. In an information age, the most notorious, outrageous, oppositional statements clamor for our attention. Even in education, such polarized debates can be misinterpreted as learning. In words that seem even more applicable and insightful today than when she wrote them, Deborah Tannen (1998) posited that:

> The argument culture urges us to approach the world—and the people living in it—in an adversarial frame of mind. It rests on the assumption that opposition is the best way to get anything done: The best way to discuss an idea is to set up a debate; the best way to cover news is to find spokespeople who express the most extreme, polarized views and present them as "both sides" . . . the best way to show you are really thinking is to criticize. (pp. 3–4)

Tannen also notes, "Although criticizing is surely part of critical thinking, it is not synonymous with it" (p. 273). As we read, write, listen, and discuss, we will do so critically and with a dose of constructive skepticism, but rather than mere argumentation, our goal will be exploration about and across educational issues through talk and other modes.

While talk is important, Burbules (1993) makes a further distinction between talk and actual dialogue. *Dialogue is not merely talk*:

> **Dialogue** is an activity directed toward discovery and new understanding, which stands to improve the knowledge, insight, or sensitivity of its participants. . . . Dialogue represents a continuous, developmental communicative interchange through which we stand to gain a fuller apprehension of the world, ourselves, and one another. (p. 8)

If Burbules's definition sounds familiar, it may be because he echoes a key tenant of John Dewey, one of education's most esteemed scholars. Dewey also believed that educative experiences were "defined by movement, by a trajectory toward a worthy goal" (McVee, 2004, p. 897). In Book Club interactions, one of our goals is to share with one another through talk and other modes, but, more importantly, to make discoveries about what we believe, what others believe, and to explore ideas, topics, instructional practices, feelings, and information that we may not have ever encountered. Discovery is an essential process of exploration because choices we make about teaching and learning, and how we will position students, are grounded in cultural belief systems.

In entering into Book Clubs that explore issues of language, literacy, and culture through narrative, our overarching goal is to help educators acquire and construct new knowledge and to work toward change. Discussions of literature, our own narratives, ethnography, autobiography, and research, become part of a learning process in which we assert our own beliefs (both those based on lived experience and those grounded in what we have read or heard from others). As Burbules (1993) has also observed:

> When we assert a belief that we hold, we also offer an implied promise to provide at least some of the evidence and reasons behind that belief, if asked. We may not be asked; we may not be able to provide those reasons fully; and we may not convince others if we do—but by making the assertion we commit ourselves to that broader obligation. (p. 75)

This means that rather than speaking from the standpoint of belief, we will look to course texts for evidence that supports our opinions and be prepared to provide explication and justification—even if our explanations are not as articulate or fully developed as we would like. Burbules eloquently paraphrases what one of Mary's former professors often stated upfront in his seminars: "Half-baked ideas are welcome." This means that dialogue is not so much about having the right answer or showing how smart we are or about defending our territory, but about putting out a substantive idea—even one that we may not yet be able to fully articulate.

openess to ideas

Note too that dialogue is also about obligation. Professing an opinion or stating a response is not the end point. Rather we are obligated to further examine, explore, consider, challenge, question, and even to think against our own ideas in the company of others. Finding evidence and sustaining an open, exploratory stance is an essential part of evidence-based thinking and critical interactions with text. These actions also require hard work, and to be honest, such explorations often involve a certain amount of discomfort or risk.

REFLECTION POINT

Consult Appendix A at the end of this chapter and spend some time thinking about the question: What makes for effective dialogue and discussion?

Learning from the Best of Game Play: Moving Away from Dialogue as the Doubting Game and Toward Dialogue as the Believing Game

Futurist and game designer Jane McGonigal (2011) suggests that our world—our physical reality—is broken. Hunger, poverty, global warming, health care, education, and other challenges continue to create problems around the globe. But, McGonigal has a radical proposition: we need to play more games. She observes that for centuries human beings have been engaging in game play as a creative and constructive activity. McGonigal's unique idea is that games, even video or virtual reality games, do not have to be a waste of time. In contrast, she suggests that engaging in social, collaborative, and creative game play in virtual and embodied environments can help us find ways of fixing our broken reality.

McGonigal's assertion is appealing to us, in part, because we know that there are some educational challenges that are long-standing. For example, the correlation between poverty and the risk of school failure is well documented and can influence the literacy development of children and the resources that children have access to (e.g., see Neuman & Celano, 2012). Gender and race also correlate strongly with higher drop-out rates and being labeled at-risk (Edwards, McMillon, & Turner, 2010).

We don't have McGonigal's resources as a game designer; she designs games that take place in virtual spaces, but also in real time—physical spaces that can have hundreds of participants. Despite our limitations, we do have the ability to adopt a gamelike mindset in our conversations and interactions. Here, the word "game" is used in the best sense, not just to win a point or score against an opponent, but to engage in conversational play or even multimodal composition using a stance that results in learning, much the same way that children use games and play to learn about the world.

Consider that many of us are well schooled in playing what Peter Elbow calls the doubting game, particularly in academic settings (2005). If we are asked to read an article or are introduced to a new teaching method, we raise questions, critique, or look for holes. Clearly, this is important because we want educators to be thoughtful, questioning individuals. But, when we ascribe to the doubting game, we approach a set of readings, topics, or ideas primed to look for what is wrong. Such questioning, while important, if it is our most frequent stance, leaves us with little of substance to move a conversation (or learning) forward. As an alternative, Elbow proposes that we suspend disbelief or critique momentarily, and play the believing game (2008).

"The believing game," observes Tannen (1998), "is still a game. It simply asks you to give it a whirl: Read as if you believed, and see where it takes you. Then you can go back and ask whether you want to accept or reject elements in the argument or the whole argument or idea" (p. 273). The point here is not that we should stop doubting, but that critique or doubt should not be the sum of our response. *Critique or criticism is not the same as critical thinking.* Our most difficult and worthy challenge may not be critiquing a viewpoint with which we disagree. Rather, the greatest challenge may lie in working toward a nuanced understanding of another's belief, particularly if his or her views make us uncomfortable. Or even in learning how to critique or examine our own opinions.

We may not be able to completely understand another's view, particularly if we disagree, but in trying to suspend doubt at least momentarily, we take a step toward one another rather than an additional step away from one another. This willingness to engage with others, hear them out, and respect the art of dialogue is a fundamental element of a democratic society.

Jenny, Jan, Rachel, and Stacy Play the Doubting Game

The excerpt below focuses on European American teachers Jenny, Jan, Rachel, and Stacy, who are members of a Book Club group. Rachel, Stacey, and Jan are in their mid-twenties, and Jenny is in her mid-forties. They are talking about the book *White Teacher*, written by Vivian Paley (1979/2000) about her experiences as a child-centered teacher working to understand her own racial identity as a White (but also Jewish) teacher of children of various racial and ethnic backgrounds. A major theme in Paley's book was her own "colorblindness"—thinking that the best way to deal with racial difference was to avoid any mention or acknowledgement of difference. Paley (2000)[1] also explains in her book that her colorblind attitude toward race ultimately revealed problems in how she positioned all children around their differences: "My awkwardness with black children was not a singular phenomenon. It uncovered a serious flaw in my relationship with all children" (p. xix). Paley revoiced the words of Mrs. Hawkins, an African American parent. Mrs. Hawkins drew Paley's attention to the positive differences of race by stating: "What you value, you talk about" (p. 131). Although some may find Paley's book dated, two of its strengths that withstand the test of time are her raw honesty and her deep devotion to a child-centered classroom.

The many books Paley has written make it clear that she is a responsive teacher, and she clearly understands and seeks to understand children (Paley, 1986). At the time Paley originally published *White Teacher*, she and other educators were optimistic about integrating schools and eliminating the legacies of desegregation and racial animosity. Sadly, many decades after the Supreme Court barred *de jure* segregation (segregation protected by law), many cities and schools have experienced *de facto* segregation (segregation due to poverty or history or other factors). While not supported by law, such de facto segregation has limited certain populations and people groups to particular areas, effectively creating segregated communities and schools.

Initially, in the discussion group, members started their conversation noting that they did not like the book. While their responses are harsh, keep in mind that this group of students had already developed a rapport with one another through previous Book Clubs. Also, across the semester, we should note that all of these students did have moments when they actively engaged with course materials in thoughtful ways. Their unwillingness to consider the benefits of Paley's knowledge is not representative of their learning as a whole across the semester.

This night Jenny starts the discussion:

Jenny: I have to tell you, this was the saddest book I have ever read. There were some redeeming points, but oh my God. When she went on . . .

Jan: I don't even know if it was worth being published.

Stacy: I don't think it was worth my fourteen, sixteen dollars or something. I really . . . take this off of the syllabus.

Stacy's quip pretty much sums up the group's feelings about the book—definitely not worth the money, not worth reading. Group members continue in this vein for a few minutes, critiquing Paley's approach to teaching in a child-centered way through a lot of child-centered activity and play (e.g., "Yeah, the play centers are fine and dandy, but not once did I hear her try to teach"). They are critical of Paley's exploration of her own stance as a White teacher (e.g. "She just kept on saying, like, she doesn't have any knowledge of Black people. What is wrong with being a White teacher? I mean, I'm a White teacher. I don't see anything wrong with it"). Group members even criticized the book cover and referring to the "grandma on the cover," noting "There aren't that many teachers that old." At this point, the group did not realize that this photo was an image of Paley with some of her own students. These student responses seem firmly anchored in the "culture of critique" in order to pass judgment (Tannen, 1998, p. 277).

These comments also demonstrate a profound misreading of Paley's text and intentions as an educator. Group members mistake Paley's child-centered approach and focus on the child as a starting point as a failure to teach. The position here is one of judgment of Paley's teaching ability and style. The group mistakes Paley's honest description of her own "errors and omissions" in teaching as her just saying she doesn't have knowledge of Black people (p. xvi). The stance by group members here is one of defensiveness around race: "What is wrong with being a White teacher?" There is also overt ageism in the discussion of the "grandma" on the cover, with the assumption that this older woman could not represent modern-day teachers. Implicit in this stance is that part of Paley's problem is that she is just "old."

Interestingly, it is Jenny, who essentially started this negative thread, who wades into the sea of criticism and doubt and who begins playing the believing game by introducing the idea that the group should perhaps entertain the notion that something could be gained from Paley's book.

How Jenny Introduces the Believing Game

REFLECTION POINT: READ THE QUESTIONS BELOW. USE THE QUESTIONS TO GUIDE YOUR ANALYSIS OF THIS GROUP'S DISCUSSION

1. What do you notice about the pattern of Jenny's speech at the beginning of her first turn of talk?
2. What does she say that she did? Why did she do this?
3. What did she learn?
4. How did other group members respond? How do you interpret their remarks?

Jenny: You know, I'll tell ya, I did something when reading this book that . . . believe it or not—you don't have to believe me—I didn't do it until I read this book. I'm not saying that I don't see color 'cause you see it, but you get to a point where you don't think about it because I have too many other things to think about. After reading this book, I went in and I counted my students. There are six White people in the class including me and there's like 26 people in there, or 25, and the rest are all African Americans. I went, "Oh my God." And I really didn't realize it, but reading this book started me thinking, and I don't want to think like that [color blind], you know? And . . . because I don't. I don't . . . it's not that I don't see the difference, but I don't want to deal with race. . . .

Stacy: Well, they should come to you and say, "Oh, it's time to go to our White teacher now." Do you think they see you as, "Oh, hey, time for this class, we're going to see . . ."

Jan: Time to go see "Whitey."

Jenny: I did a survey with my kids.

Rachel: Change your nametag on the door to "White teacher."

Jenny: And this is very interesting. For my creative part [of my Book Log], one of the questions [I asked my eighth graders] was, "Do you feel uncomfortable dealing with White teachers?" One girl said, "No, I'm half that color." "No, I don't feel uncomfortable because that's racism." "No, I think it's okay. There's nothing big about dealing with another color. We are all the same, it doesn't matter what color we are." "No, because it doesn't matter what color you are." "No, because there is nothing wrong. They're teachers. They're just like other people." Not really. "No, because I have White in my own blood." Not one thought it was a big deal. In fact, one girl said, "Gee, I never thought of that." I mean, they [students] know we [teachers] are White.

Rachel: And also, what are they exposed to? You know, a majority of teachers . . . I don't know the numbers, but, I mean, you see a lot of teachers are White. You don't see a lot of Black teachers.

Jenny: We have a staff of 50 plus, including aides and teachers and there's only three African Americans, um . . .

Following this excerpt, Jenny and her classmates broaden their discussion to include racial and gendered make up of schools. They observe that in many schools in their urban community the overwhelming majority of students are Black, but the majority of teachers are White. They further observe that there are even fewer Black male teachers and few male teachers in general in their elementary- and middle-school settings. Although their explorations are somewhat tentative and underdeveloped, they begin to explore what it might mean that certain genders (males) and certain racial groups (African Americans) are underrepresented in the teaching corps. Through this additional conversation, the group does actually begin to engage in dialogue as activity directed toward new understanding. Their conversation is a mix of brutally honest first responses about

Paley and some negative feelings toward the book, followed by Jenny's description of how she gave a survey to her students. What results is an odd mix. On the one hand there is the scathing criticism that couples with Jenny's own attempt to show evidence that colorblindness does not exist in her school. Ultimately, it is Jenny's asking, "Could this maybe be true? Do we not see race?" that ultimately scaffolds the group to arrive at the place where they begin a dialogue. Let's take a closer look at the excerpt above.

Did you notice how Jenny's initial comments are framed to bring her group members on board? She says she "did something" when reading this book and tells her group they don't have to believe her (e.g., Jenny looked around her classroom of 25–26 people, and there were six White people and 20 or 21 Black people). Although Jenny doubts Paley's admonishment that White teachers often ascribe to colorblindness as a means to not thinking about race, Jenny considers that she too has fallen into this stance. She even admits, "It's not that I don't see the difference, but I don't want to deal with race. . . ." It is an interesting position that Jenny, who purports that Paley has nothing to teach her, is reawakened to seeing difference in the classroom while reading Paley. Jenny even reacts by counting how may White students and how many Black students were in her classroom. "I went in, and I counted my students . . . I went 'Oh my God.'" Jenny uses her class to gather evidence that the text/Paley is incorrect, that race doesn't matter, and to vindicate her notion that not seeing color is acceptable.

Notice, too, how Jenny's group responds to her comments. Although the tenor of the conversation is difficult to assess on paper without all the multimodal elements (e.g., prosody, pitch, intonation, etc.), Jenny's group treats her revelation with neither praise nor disdain. Instead, they use a playful banter to lighten the moment. Implicit in their comments: "Time to go see Whitey" and "Change your nametag on the door to 'White teacher'" is a humorous take on the role of the White teacher and of whiteness. This humor functions a number of ways. It helps to take a serious, heavy matter and lessen its weight. It allows Jan, Stacy, and Rachel a way to maintain face in the conversation without having to point out to Jenny that she is departing from the book-bashing talk that started their conversation, and seems to be suggesting a way that Paley actually prompted some important thinking. Most interestingly, after Jenny introduces this topic shift and describes the responses from students in her class, the group begins its most substantive conversation of the evening: A discussion of what it means to have teachers who do not have the same racial, ethic, or gendered identity as the students.

Let us be clear. We are not saying that the group has arrived, that Paley's work is not of value, or that this is the best way to have a thoughtful conversation about Paley's work. Indeed, interpretations of this transcript other than what we have presented above are possible. For example, Jenny is likely using her students' responses, in part, to legitimize deemphasizing race as an essential sociocultural component of her classroom context. Also, her statement, ". . . but you get to a point where you don't think about it [race] because I have too many other things to think about" implies that "other things," such as the everyday activities of teaching students to read, write, and calculate numbers, are important while racial identity is not important. Other participants may be using humor to help mask their own feelings or discomfort about having attention called to their own racial backgrounds or their own unwillingness to speak out.

The value of the dialogue does not come because we can identify that participants have arrived at an end point in their learning. We would argue that the group has begun a conversation; they have begun to engage in a *dialogue* around some critical topics. The merit of this discussion is that the group has enacted a starting point for a substantive discussion that can continue on into other contexts. They have begun to play the believing game by asking: What if this could be true?

Jenny Continues to Play the Believing Game

Perhaps more than any other student, Jenny demonstrated the tensions between the doubting game and the believing game. Like many White teachers who are introduced to uncomfortable topics around racial inequality, poverty, de facto segregation, and the intersection of these issues with literacy development, Jenny often responded defensively. This defensiveness is represented in statements such as: "It's not that I'm a conservative . . ." or "I felt, as a White teacher, I was being attacked. Strong language, I know, but that is how I felt" or faulting an author for "teacher bashing." Time and again, Jenny responded in the voice of what Finn (2009, p. 8) calls "the hard bitten" schoolteacher—practical, down-to-earth, grounded in the "What will this do for me Monday morning?" mode of thought. But, to her credit, Jenny seldom, if ever, stalled out at that point. Repeatedly, she would mull over what she had read or discussed, sometimes in anger, and always with plain-spoken honesty. Having gotten out her initial, emotional responses, Jenny had an interesting way of reconsidering these initial responses from a more distanced, objective position. In doing this, Jenny would describe the process of how she was rethinking her views, or even changing them. She did not change because her course instructor convinced her, but because, much like Paley, she would go directly to the children in her classroom to test out various ideas espoused by authors we had studied. This "trying out" involved different tasks, ranging from designing and giving a cultural survey to her students to changing the curriculum of the classroom to be more inclusive of all races, nationalities, and ethnic groups.

Near the end of the semester, Jenny shared one particularly relevant example. In keeping with her frank, no-nonsense approach, she stated her purpose was to show that this multicultural stuff was not "just a bunch of crap."

After reading Ladson-Billings' (1994/2009) book *The Dreamkeepers: Successful Teachers of African American Children*, Jenny had said she "couldn't relate" to it. As a White teacher, she felt that Ladson-Billings was "attacking" her. But, after her anger died down, she took a step back and began to reflect on her teaching. In her Book Log she listed a number of hard-hitting self-directed questions followed by a statement that she would try to make great strides in the area of cultural relevancy in her classroom. During class discussion of *Dreamkeepers*, Jenny struggled with the portraits of teachers and teaching that Ladson-Billings used to illustrate the need for culturally relevant pedagogy. Because Jenny taught in an urban, mostly Puerto Rican neighborhood but lived in another community, she was particularly skeptical of the assertion that teachers should live in and be active in the their students' communities. Yet Jenny continued to engage with Ladson-Billings even beyond the actual talk of the university classroom. Partly in defense of her own teaching and partly out of curiosity, Jenny decided to give her students a cultural survey that she designed.

When Jenny had given the cultural survey, it happened to be Black history month, and one student asked: "Why do we always study Black culture and history? Why don't we ever study Puerto Rico?" Jenny puzzled over this, and because she was in an eighth-grade social studies classroom, she decided to let the students study Puerto Rico. Each week she came to our university class with updates on what her students were learning and doing, and she reported on things that surprised her. "Did you know that you can go to three bookstores before you find a map or a book on Puerto Rico?" During another discussion, she reported that, on a whim, she stopped at a Puerto Rican restaurant near the school. It turned out that one of her student's father ran the restaurant. Angel excitedly introduced his father to his teacher; this amazed Jenny because Angel was sometimes difficult to deal with in school. Because Angel and his classmates were nearing the end of the Puerto Rico unit, Angel's father agreed to bring in some Puerto Rican food. Jenny observed that this simple connection was a way to begin getting to know the community and the people in it.

Jenny also relayed other students' responses to changes in the curriculum. In her typical frank speech, she described how one student, usually "a real pain in my ass," had dramatically shifted his behavior during this particular unit. By encouraging students to bring their culture into the classroom through their connections to their own families, histories, and discourse practices and through the more visible trappings of culture (e.g., the language, music, dance, and food), Jenny assured her classmates and Book Club group that it "made a difference" to the students. As she learned more about her students and their local knowledge, Jenny felt more connected to her students and more a part of their lives. Part of what she was coming to realize was that her students were embodied individuals. They could not leave their racial, ethnic, linguistic, cultural, or religious (or many other) identities at the classroom door. As they walked through the world, and through the school door, they carried all of these identities with them.

This was clearly a powerful experience for Jenny. We wish that we could say every teacher in the class had such an experience. Unfortunately, there were some, even some teachers who were teaching in similar schools, who continued to play the doubting game. To these few participants, the authors of course texts were unrealistic, even clueless. These participants continued to play the doubting game as represented by comments such as: "Those parents don't really care about their kids." "Those kids are too far behind to catch up." "Maybe if Mom would check his homework, he could learn something." "Racism doesn't really exist anymore."

Interestingly, for Jenny, even approximately 18 months after the conclusion of the course, she could still recall some of her strong feelings. She recalled:

> That class—that course—made me start to think. . . . I felt like I was, I remember this, I felt like I was being attacked. . . . [*Pausing to reread part of her Ladson-Billings Book Log.*]. You know, but like I said in here, I found myself questioning my own teaching. Am I a culturally relevant teacher?
>
> I believe all the readings [in the course] say the same thing. In their own way, every article and book stresses the importance of listening to our students. By listening, I mean paying strict attention to what they bring to the classroom. By listening, I mean valuing who they are and where they come from. By listening, I mean embracing all our students' cultural identities by instituting a culturally relevant educational experience.

In this chapter we have used Jenny's discussions, Book Logs, and actions to demonstrate that she has started an engaged dialogue not only with others, but she has started an internal and continuing dialogue within herself. Remembering Burbules's (1993) assertion that dialogue is not merely talk, Jenny has started to embark on a path toward discovery and new understandings of her students as well as herself. If Jenny continues to develop an engaged dialogue as she listens to her students, her work and efforts may prove fruitful for herself as well as her students as she becomes a more reflective and effective teacher. Jenny pointed out the importance of listening in the process of dialogic engagement. In Chapter 6, we take a closer look at listening in Book Clubs and dialogic interactions.

note

Note

1. All Paley quotes are from the 2000 edition.

References

Burbules, N. C. (1993). *Dialogue in teaching: Theory and practice.* New York: Teachers College Press.

Dewey, J. (1938). *Experience and education.* New York: Macmillan.

Edwards, P.A., McMillon, G.T., & Turner, J.D. (2010). *Change is gonna come: Transforming literacy education for African American students.* New York: Teachers College Press/International Reading Association.

Elbow, P. (2005). Bringing the rhetoric of assent and the believing game together—and into the classroom. *College English, 67*(4), 388–399.

Elbow, P. (2008). The believing game—Methodological believing. Retrieved from http://works.bepress.com/peter_elbow/20

Finn, P. (2009). *Literacy with an attitude*. Albany: State University of New York.

Ladson-Billings, G. (1994/2009). *The dreamkeepers: Successful teachers of African American children*. San Francisco: Jossey-Bass Publishers.

McGonigal, J. (2011). *Reality is broken*. New York: The Penguin Press.

McVee, M.B. (2004). Narrative and the exploration of culture in teachers' discussions of literacy, identity, self and other. *Teaching and Teacher Education, 20*(8), 881–899.

Neuman, S.B., & Celano, D.C. (2012). *Giving our children a fighting chance: Poverty, literacy, and the development of information capital*. New York: Teachers College Press.

Paley, V. (1986). On listening to what the children say. *Harvard Educational Review, 56*(2), 122–131.

Paley, V. (1979/2000). *White teacher*. Cambridge, MA: Harvard University Press.

Tannen, D. (1998). *The argument culture: Stopping America's war of words*. New York: Ballantine Publishing Group.

Appendix A

Application Principle

Preparing for or Improving Your Book Club Discussion Group

Try This Activity: What Constitutes Effective Dialogue and Discussion?

1. (**Think**) Based on what you know about Book Club, consider this question in which children or youth are the Book Club participants. It may help to have a particular age or grade level in mind: What would constitute an effective discussion if children or youth were the participants? That is, how would teachers know when a "good" discussion was occurring? Write down your ideas in list form.

   a. Now look at your list: What elements of a "good book club discussion for kids" would also apply to this question: What makes for an effective/educational discussion for adults? Add an asterisk ★ or highlight those elements that also apply to adults.

   b. Next add to your list. Think specifically about adult discussions (i.e., a book club where adults form the participants): Are there things that adults could or should do that children or youth would or could not do? Add these to your list. Keep in mind that "Dewey (1938) felt that educative experiences were defined by movement, by a trajectory toward a worthy goal" (McVee, 2004, p. 897) and that our goal in Book Club is dialogue.

2. (**Pair**) Compare your list with someone else. Feel free to add ideas you may have missed to your list.

3. (**Think**) In a Book Club group, what are some specific words or phrases you can use to help your discussion group facilitate dialogue? (e.g., "Well, getting

back to the book. . . . I'm not sure I agree with you, but tell me more about how you made that connection . . .)

4. (**Share**) With your Book Club or other small group (e.g. 3–4 participants), focus on the issues surrounding an adult peer-led discussion group. Share the items on your list that you feel are important for an educative discussion. Talk about what you think fosters a dialogue among participants.

5. (**Extension**) Electronic spaces (e.g., wikis, forums, shared electronic documents, Google docs, etc.) work great for sharing ideas. Work with your group to choose elements that your group feels are most important to fostering dialogue in Book Club. As you continue with your discussions, revisit this page and update it with comments and questions.

Once you have completed this activity, consult Appendix B: Strategies for Book Club Discussion.

Appendix B

Strategies for Book Club Discussion: What particular words or phrases could you use to help your Book Club group establish or maintain an effective or educative dialogue? (Book Club participants who were preservice and inservice teachers generated the following items, and these are used with their permission.)

Redirecting/Shifting Conversation:

Let's regroup.
Let's refocus.
Let's see. What should we focus on next?
I'm wondering if we could just stop for one minute and write down what we are thinking and share those ideas to help our conversation move forward.
Have a signal to stop the conversation
As I was saying earlier . . .
We haven't heard what [person name] thinks. What are your thoughts?
Let's consider this from all sides . . .

Connections:

Can we tie this experience (your experience) to our reading?
Hmm. . . . that reminds me of . . . (something about the literature)
What did you think about . . . (and reference text, event, person in text, etc.)?
How did you feel when . . . happened?

What would you do if . . . (what happened in book) happened to you?
If you were [person in the book], what would you do next?
When I read . . . it made me think about . . .

Deeper Explorations:

What did the author mean . . . (and reference text or page number)?
What did you think about . . . (and reference text, event, person in text, etc.)?
I have a suggestion, could we all look through the book for a favorite quote
    (or a quote) to discuss?
I'm sort of struggling with this . . .
When I read . . . it made me think about . . .
Was this book compelling to you? Why or why not?
How can you relate that . . . back to what [person name] said about . . .
What connections do you see specifically to other texts or articles we have
    read?
What can we learn from this?

Considerations of Writing Style:

What do you think about the author's style of writing?
Was the writing style in this book interesting to you? Why or why not?
Here's a passage I thought was powerful writing. Can we talk about what
    makes it powerful or if you agree/disagree?

6

THE RELATIONSHIP BETWEEN WORDS

Learning the Art of Listening

PRE-READING ACTIVITY

Watch the first 11 minutes of "The Birth of a Word" by Deb Roy (2011) on TED Talks at www.ted.com/talks/deb_roy_the_birth_of_a_word.
   Then consider the questions below.

1.   What do you notice about your own listening as you view Professor Roy's talk?
2.   What can you infer about the child's listening in the video? About the caregiver's listening?
3.   What do you observe about interactions between the caregivers and the child?
4.   What do you notice about the physical spaces in the video and the role of the body?

On Beginning to Consider Listening

In "The Birth of a Word," Deb Roy tracks the first word spoken by his son as a toddler. What is remarkable about Roy's research is that it captures in image, in sound, and through representation and schematics how learning is situated in real-world embodied interactions. The son is listening and taking in language, but he is also acting within the environment through all of his physical senses—the types of embodied learning we referred to in Chapter 4. In fact, scientists know that before we are born we are listening, because unborn babies respond to a mother's voice. So even before Roy's son was born, this little guy was listening in! Another way to think of this is in the parlance of John Dewey (1896), who noted that organisms do not just take in information and respond (the old stimulus–response theory of learning). Dewey observed that there is a transactional space surrounding any organism; this space encompasses the environment–organism transaction. To put this in less academic terms, in Roy's video we see a young child and the environment surrounding that child. The child learns through interaction with the environment and with others within that environment—that is, in the transactional space between child and environment.

Across the lifespan, we experience many more of these transactional learning events. While we cannot capture all of these external environments and bring them into the classroom, one of the ways we can tap into these embodied experiences is by putting ourselves into storylines that position us to explore the worlds and experiences of others. This is part of what Jenny talked about in reading books about the life experiences of others. Jenny also tapped into others' transactional experiences by taking action on what she had read and asking for others' input. We tend to think of listening as a passive activity, but Jenny also listened to what she was hearing from her students, from her peers in class, and from authors whose works she read. Listening was one of the key actions Jenny demonstrated.

In the previous chapter, we discussed how Jenny set aside her own evaluative judgments to begin to wrestle with the deeper ideas presented by texts. Instead of merely rejecting Ladson-Billings's notion of culturally relevant pedagogy as unrealistic, or instead of simply stating presumptuously, "I already do all this," Jenny reflected deeply on those elements of the texts that troubled her. She listened to the authors of texts, her students, and members of her group for feedback as she used evidence to elaborate her views of teaching and learning. Two things are critical to recognize here. First, Jenny did not merely accept what she had read and begin to parrot it back as her own belief. She actively listened, but she also critiqued, wrestled with, and contested the texts she encountered. For Jenny, listening was never a passive act (McVee, Hopkins, & Bailey, 2011).

The first half of this chapter introduces readers to the role of listening in dialogue and explains how reflective listening is a generative process for dialogue in educational settings. Several excerpts from a Book Club discussion follow this explanation. Readers are invited to analyze how participants in these discussions interact and how participants appear to be listening.

REFLECTION QUESTIONS

1. How do you know someone is listening to you?
2. Have you ever had an experience in a book club discussion or other discussion where you felt someone wasn't listening? Why did you think someone wasn't listening?
3. What are different types of listening you participate in during the day? What types of listening are required in a book club discussion? How is listening in your book club group the same or different than listening you do in other areas?

Listening: A Generative Process for Dialogue in Educational Settings

Listening is typically part of a required curriculum. In K–12 curricula, it is often listed on scope and sequence charts for textbooks across disciplines. Listening is referred to as a key element of standards, such as Common Core, and often referenced in literacy skills (e.g., reading, writing, listening, speaking). While often included, listening is seldom addressed directly, whereas reading, writing, and even classroom discussion may be attended to more directly. One reason listening may receive less attention is because many of our listening skills are tacit and not easily observed. In contrast, we can easily observe someone reading, hear and see how fluent they are, or see what they are producing if they are writing.

By the time children are of school age, they are often reminded to, "Be quiet and listen." Within schools, students are typically asked to demonstrate listening as a behavior (e.g., sitting quietly, keeping eyes on a speaker, repeating information, etc.). While students may spend a great deal of time listening, especially in classrooms where teaching methods are traditional, overall listening does not receive as much direct attention as reading and writing. Even within books for adult educators, listening is less often referred to as the primary means of actively constructing and producing knowledge but is more typically implied as the counterpart in classroom discussions and seldom discussed directly (Haroutunian-Gordon, 2010). But, as obvious as it may seem, we cannot have dialogue without listening.

With regard to listening, Rice and Burbules (2010) suggest that

> Listening can be profoundly educative. It is one of the principal ways in which we learn about the world and its people, develop a sense of self, form relations with others, and expand our moral and intellectual capacities. The

extent to which listening can be educative in these and other ways depends not only on the content of listening, as important as that is, but also on the qualities we bring to listening and that we develop in the course of listening. Learning to listen well is educationally generative. (p. 2740)

It is probably easier for most of us to think of talk as generative; when we talk it is easy to hear and to see that we are producing something. We may think of writing or reading in similar ways. However, when considered from the stand-point of embodied learning, discussion is not just a strategy to talk about content; discussion is enactive. Words acquire their meanings in action and activity—think of the toddler in the video that opened this chapter and all the activities he was participating in that grounded the word "water."

Without meanings grounded in experience, words are empty shells. Any youngster who has learned to try out swearing in another language can attest to this. Someone might tell you that a certain word has a vulgar meaning, but in another language, at least initially, we can swear completely without reservation because there is no history of certain words as "bad," "taboo," "secret," "vulgar," or otherwise forbidden. We say these words and hear them, but in terms of listening for meanings, their meanings are not grounded in experience. We might say that devoid of their deep, rich, contextual meanings, these words are but empty shells.

There is a parallel in conversation to the "words as empty shells" analogy. There are numerous individuals who, through the Internet, television, and even radio, still share extreme polarizing rhetoric around political, social, and cultural issues. These are examples of what Tannen (see Chapter 5) characterized as "the argu-ment culture" where the point is to win at all costs. Rather than thoughtful, care-fully considered explorations of issues, the point is to hammer home an ideology. For example, on many popular television shows where politics are "discussed," even a cursory examination reveals that those on opposite sides of an issue may spend as much time talking over one another and interrupting as they do actually exploring an issue. While these individuals have mastered language-in-use, their verbal banter seldom represents dialogic engagement where new ideas and new learning occurs. Rather, these verbal engagements are more like empty shells of conversation. People talk but seldom listen deeply.

One of the reasons why this should matter to teachers, especially those who work and teach in democratic societies, is that we are connected socially, politi-cally, historically, and culturally to many people who may be very unlike us. We may not share the same individual ideals, cultural norms, values, ideologies, or practices. While a great deal of *de facto* segregation may exist, for example, within the US and other countries, it is also the case that schools are unique spaces where incredibly diverse populations can come together. As such, schools more than any other entity provide the opportunity to teach children, youth, and even the adults who mentor and teach them how to engage in civil discourse and deeply dialogic discussion. Parker (2010) states this dialogic engagement as a requirement in soci-eties where governance is meant to be shared:

[A] society aspiring to political community of this kind needs an education system that inducts young people into a civic culture of speaking and listening to people they might not know or like, whose behavior and beliefs they may not warm to, with whom they may be unequally related due to histories of discrimination and servitude, and with whom they may have no occasion otherwise to be in discussion, or even in the same room, but with whom they must be involved in political discussions—governance—on the public's problems. (p. 2817)

In order to carry out discussions in a dialogic spirit, we must practice listening with compassion and empathy, but also with a reflective stance. Listening involves hearing words and phrases to understand meaning but also to infer and interpret meanings and consider what sense to make of these.

Reflective Listening

Consistently, we ask children from certain communities to speak two ways. Although I may not speak two ways, it would be a good thing to hear two ways, multiple ways.

Karen Hankins, *Teaching Through the Storm* (2003, p. 45)

Hankins wrote these words about a tumultuous year in her teaching life in which she spent a great deal of time writing and reflecting through narrative to help gain insights into the children in her classroom. Hankins observed that her teaching journal had "become a place of reflection and dissection on my own long-held perspectives on teaching, learning, and children" (p. 1). In her book-length work, Hankins shares her intimate reflections on teaching and children, and it is worth pausing to consider: What is reflection?

In their work with literacy teachers, Shanahan and her colleagues (Shanahan et al., 2013) developed and applied a definition of reflection to the practices of literacy teachers, stating that reflection is

a goal-directed process that moves teachers to identify a situation, process, or experience that is puzzling, interesting, celebratory, or otherwise intriguing and view it through multiple lenses. Developing particular skill sets or dispositions is necessary for reflection, but a particular set of skills or dispositions is not sufficient to become a reflective practitioner. Reflective teachers strive to gain strategic knowledge of a situation in order to develop and explore questions, recognize, or acknowledge complexity of situations, processes or experiences, and make adaptations to their actions, beliefs, positions, and classroom and pedagogical practices. Reflection is interpretive in that individuals bring their knowledge and experiences to the situation. Reflection is self-directed and collaborative in nature. (p. 305)

While Shanahan and her colleagues applied this definition of reflection to practice, particularly the pedagogical practices that literacy teachers used in learning to teach struggling readers, we can also consider reflection in terms of listening. In *Teaching Through the Storm*, Hankins repeatedly demonstrates how she as teacher must listen first, and as she says in the opening quote, listen in "multiple ways" (Hankins, 2003, p. 45). In *reflective listening*, participants in a dialogic interaction can listen to

- Identify a situation, process, or experience that is puzzling, interesting, celebratory, or otherwise intriguing and view this situation through multiple lenses;
- Develop a specific skill or set of dispositions;
- Gain strategic knowledge of a situation in order to develop and explore questions and to recognize or acknowledge complexity of situations, processes, or experiences;
- Make adaptations to actions, beliefs, positions, and classroom and pedagogical practices;
- Interpret situations based on their own knowledge but also collaborate with others to interpret situations based on collaborative knowledge;
- Reflective listening should also include "reverent listening" in order to
- Show "awe and wonder" with regard to subject matter and students;
- Demonstrate "deep respect for their students while seeking to deserve their respect";
- Enact "strong leadership" while including others in deliberations of leadership;
- "understand the importance of ritual and ceremony in establishing classroom and school community" (Rud & Garrison, 2010, p. 2780; for a more complete list see Appendix A).

Reflective and reverent listening facilitates dialogue by building not only positive receptive experiences, but also by building in a transactional aspect to listening. Listening can assist us in playing the believing game and help us to avoid the empty shells of rhetoric based in the doubting game or extreme skepticism and cynicism.

REFLECTION POINT

1. Look at the lists above and in Appendix A for reflective listening and reverent listening.
2. Think of an example from a teacher who demonstrated reverent/reflective listening. This can be from your own experience as a student or from a teacher you have read about or viewed in a film.

3. How do you know that the teacher demonstrated reverent/reflective listening? In particular, what elements listed above did the teacher convey or exemplify?
4. Have you ever demonstrated elements of reverent/reflective listening as a teacher (think of the word "teacher" here broadly)? Which ones? How did you enact this type of listening?
5. How can reflective/reverent listening help us see things from others' perspectives?

Playing the Doubting Game, the Rhetoric of Skepticism, and the Art of Listening

In the first part of this chapter, we have looked at some of the hallmarks of reflective or reverent listening. In the remainder of the chapter, we look at several examples of talk from a group that is struggling to engage in dialogue and struggling to listen. Our purpose here is to help guide readers through a close reading and analysis of group talk to identify patterns of engagement and also as a means of repairing or engaging differently.

In the segment of talk below, Janice, Krissy, Mary Ann, and Ted discuss a series of articles they were asked to read for one night of their graduate seminar in language, literacy, and culture. Three of the participants, Krissy, Mary Ann, and Ted, were European American. Janice was biracial, European American and African American. Two participants, Mary Ann and Ted, had experience as teachers in schools, whereas Krissy was recently certified but did not have classroom experience. Janice was exploring teaching as a career option and had been a substitute teacher. Mary Ann, Ted, and Janice were closer in age, being in their middle to late twenties. Krissy was in her early twenties, having been homeschooled and starting an undergraduate degree at 17.

The required readings on this night included two academic articles. One article was by Kathy Au (1998) and discussed a conceptual framework using social constructivism to help understand school literacy learning for students of diverse backgrounds. The other was an article now considered a classic by many scholars. This article by Lisa Delpit (1988) discusses a literacy controversy related to teaching using skills–based approaches (such as phonics) vs. meaning–based approaches (such as whole language) to teach African American students. However, a major premise of the article, and one often less acknowledged, is that the knowledge and experiences of African American teachers have often been marginalized by their White colleagues and by White researchers. The dialogue of these Black educators has become a "silenced dialogue," because their dialogue has been excluded, silenced, or pushed to the margins where White educators do not listen.

In addition to the required readings, the participants were asked to choose two additional articles. One choice, an article by Harris (1992), focused on beliefs about literacy as viewed historically within the African American community. The other two articles (Walker-Dalhouse, 1992; Zarnowski, 1988) focused on practitioners using multicultural literature in their classrooms. (Abstracts of these articles are in Appendix B).

As you will see, there is a lot of talk going on in this transcript, but how much of this talk is dialogic? How carefully are participants listening? What kind of listening are they doing? How much do people appear to be learning? Although there are some important topics that arise for discussion, the group seems to have difficulty actually engaging in dialogic talk and active listening. Several in the group seem to approach the texts or other members of the group with the rhetoric of skepticism rather than as individuals willing to play the believing game. Again, we remind readers that these examples are from one night of talk across a 15-week semester. Not every conversation unfolded as do the excerpts below.

Analyzing Discussion for Listening and Dialogic Interaction

One of the ways we learn about talk and listening is by carefully exploring examples of talk. Rather than us telling you exactly what to see below, we feel it is helpful for you to analyze this talk. This section will guide you through an analysis of the group's talk and listening. In a world in which a constant media barrage gives us snippets of short talk as sound bites, we also feel it is important to provide you with a longer transcript. Below we have several shorter transcript excerpts. But in Appendix B, we have provided you with an extended transcript. Before we begin analysis, we review some definitions from earlier chapters.

Definitions

Dialogue

> **Dialogue** is an activity directed toward discovery and new understanding, which stands to improve the knowledge, insight, or sensitivity of its participants. . . . Dialogue represents a continuous, developmental communicative interchange through which we stand to gain a fuller apprehension of the world, ourselves, and one another.
>
> (Burbules, 1993, p. 8)

When we assert a belief that we hold, we also offer an implied promise to provide at least some of the evidence and reasons behind that belief, if asked. We may not be asked; we may not be able to provide those reasons fully;

and we may not convince others if we do—but by making the assertion we commit ourselves to that broader obligation.

(Burbules, 1993, p. 75)

The Believing Game

The Believing Game or "Methodological Believing" contrasts with the **Doubting Game**, in which texts (whether written, spoken, visual, etc.) are typically approached to look for their flaws. Keep in mind that the doubting game differs from critical thinking or reflective thinking. In reflective or critical thinking, a listener engages dialogically and recursively, considering multifaceted explanations and insights. In the doubting game, a listener's first move is to go on the defensive, to poke holes, to rebut or refute. The believing game follows the method of trying to consider that an author or a speaker might be right.

> [T]he believing game is the disciplined practice of trying to be as welcoming or accepting as possible to every idea we encounter: not just listening to views different from our own and holding back from arguing with them; not just trying to restate them without bias; but actually trying to believe them. We are using believing as a tool to scrutinize and test.
>
> (Elbow, 2008, p. 1)

The believing game encourages participants to consider various positions, listen intently, and set aside their own positions momentarily.

Analysis Procedures

Read through the transcript. Often it is helpful to work in a group of four—this is ideal, but not absolutely necessary. If you can find three others to work with, you can choose to read the part of either Janice, Krissy, Mary Ann, or Ted aloud, similar to a "Reader's Theater." As you read through the transcript, take note of your observations, reactions, and questions. In this chapter, you will discuss your analysis. We will return to the talk of this group in Chapter 7 to provide further analysis of the challenging topics.

Janice, Krissy, Mary Ann, and Ted: A Group Discussion

Excerpt 1

On this night of class, students had several articles (see Appendix B for abstracts) and could choose from several others. Before the conversation (see excerpt below), the group had briefly talked about which articles were required and what they had read. The turn below started when Ted observed that he "hated" the article that Mary Ann "loved." Mary Ann continues the conversation.

1	*Mary Ann:*	We're supposed to focus on Delpit and Au.
2	*Ted:*	Oh, good then you won't mind if I hated it.
3	*Janice:*	I wrote 'Delpit and all' because it was you know…
4	*Ted:*	Required.
5	*Mary Ann:*	Which one did you hate?
6	*Janice:*	See I was gonna find a nice way to say that.
7	*Ted:*	The one that you loved [Walker-Dahlhouse].
8	*Mary Ann:*	The one that I loved? Why?
9	*Ted:*	It brought back some memories and…
10	*Mary Ann:*	Of what?
11	*Janice:*	What, what did it bring…?
12	*Mary Ann:*	Oh my gosh. I even said [in my writing] that this article
13		gives me pride as being a teacher and you're probably
14		like: What?! There's pride in you? It was all about-oh-
15		what's her name? Walker-Dahlhouse went into a school
16		and pretty much said, brought in African American
17		culture. She brought in African American culture kind
18		of unit to like to teach the students and hoping that they
19		will take away this knowledge and continue wanting to
20		know more about different culture and I really liked it
21		because…
22	*Krissy:*	(interrupting) So we're supposed to feel guilty because
23		the white male gets more money than them?
24	*Mary Ann:*	Oh, it's a male thing. Oh, okay.
25	*Ted:*	It's a white…(trails off)
26	*Janice:*	Okay I'm just listening.
27	*Krissy:*	No, because that is. The, there's like, like for example, I
28		know this one lady, she's in the high percentage who was
29		like in the highly paying women in the entire country,
30		she was in that small percentage up there, but it's even,
31		they say…(trails off)
32	*Mary Ann:*	Help me, help me. Where are we?
33	*Janice:*	What page are you on?
34	*Ted:*	I'm not on any page. I'm just talking in general.
35	*Mary Ann:*	"Using African literature to increase…" (reading from
36		Walker-Dahlhouse title)
37	*Ted:*	Get out of there. You're doing more harm than good.
38		("You" is unclear here.) (Speakers are often overlapping
39		for the next few exchanges)
40	*Mary Ann:*	No, I wanna know why…
41	*Krissy:*	No, I'm trying to understand.
42	*Janice:*	Ted, I swear to God, all I'm going to do is listen. I swear…
43		to God.

Questions for Analysis Excerpt 1

1. What indication do you get that Ted is playing the doubting game?
2. What topic does Mary Ann introduce in Line 12?
3. How does Krissy respond? How connected is this to Mary Ann's comment? What can you infer about Krissy's listening?
4. How does Mary Ann respond to Krissy? Does Mary Ann build her talk off her previous topic or off Krissy's talk? What can you infer about Mary Ann's listening?
5. In this passage, where does the talk break down?
6. What are some of the reasons why talk appears to break down?
7. Look at specific lines of talk above. How could speakers have reframed the talk to push the conversation in a more dialogic direction? Be specific. What exact things could a speaker say or do?
8. How could speakers work to repair the conversation? What exact things could a speaker say or do?

Excerpt 2

The excerpt below continues directly following the prior conversation where Mary Ann introduced a topic related to the article by Walker-Dahlhouse that described how she used a unit on African American literature. In the first excerpt, conversation was disjointed as different speakers attempted to introduce different topics and agendas for group discussion and Mary Ann does not have a chance to explain her topic. From Lines 29 to 39, speakers seem confused and speech is fragmented. In the excerpt below, Ted forges ahead with his story about student teaching.

40	*Ted:*	Okay, what happened was, now what happened was
41		when I was student teaching, I taught on the Iroquois
42		Indian. What you're talking, you learn about the Native
43		Americans is…
44	*Janice:*	That's cool.
45	*Mary Ann:*	They play Lacrosse.
46	*Ted:*	…is that the white man throughout the book brought
47		small pox and…
48	*Mary Ann:*	We killed them out.
49	*Ted:*	We killed them. We burned their buildings. We raped
50		their women.
51	*Mary Ann:*	We were horrible.
52	*Ted:*	We stole their land.
53	*Mary Ann:*	We did though.
54	*Ted:*	And one kid comes up to me and he's like, "Did we
55		ever do anything right?" like sarcastically and it's like,
56		it reminded me of this because it's like a guilt trip, like
57		you're bad…

58	*Janice:*	No, that's what it's called, I swear to God and I'm not
59		making this up. I am not making this up, it's gonna sound
60		like I am, but there is actually like, in my other class I
61		have this entire book, I swear to God and it goes both
62		ways. It goes like on both, um, a first impression. What
63		you're feeling right now is called
64	*Mary Ann:*	Survivor's guilt.
65	*Janice:*	um, white guilt. I swear to God, it's called white guilt.
66	*Krissy:*	Well, yeah.
67	*Ted:*	I wrote that down. It's like…
68	*Janice:*	No, it's literally called "white guilt." There is, I swear.
69	*Mary Ann:*	But you know what? I too have white guilt especially
70		when I thought about how I wrote this piece on how,
71		oh, when I went to school back in the eighties…
72	*Ted:*	…what about self-esteem, you know, something like that.
73		I mean I'm not a big fan of teaching self-esteem in the
74		classroom but…
75	*Krissy:*	Oh, meaning, meaning like they read these stories…
76	*Ted:*	But I mean they should at least not feel bad, you know, at
77		least go home and say I don't care, my parents were jerks.
78	*Mary Ann:*	Well you know what I call that? I call that the hidden
79		curriculum.
80	*Janice:*	But your parents…I feel bad when people, go ahead.
81	*Krissy:*	You know what part of it is? Part of it is, is, it's like, it's
82		almost like you're guilty for what your ancestors or what
83		your fathers did.
84	*Mary Ann:*	Guilt by association.

Questions for Analysis Excerpt 2

1. Consider Ted's story about student teaching.
   a. Retell Ted's story restating the actions and events he narrated.
   b. How many turns of talk does it take for Ted to completely tell the story about student teaching?
   c. How many other speakers interrupt him?
   d. Interruptions, such as comments or overlapping talk, can help build dialogic interactions or stop dialogic conversation altogether. In this conversation, are the interruptions helpful in building the conversation? What evidence supports your response?
   e. What is Ted's reason for telling the story; that is, what point does he want other speakers to take away? What content is he trying to convey?
2. Look at the exchange between Ted and Mary Ann in Lines 40–52. They appear to be talking about the same thing, even repeating some of the same phrases.
   a. Do you think they are agreeing? Support your answer with evidence.
   b. Do you think they are listening to each other? Support your answer with evidence.

3. What does Janice seek to do in Lines 56–60, 62, and 65? How effective is her introduction of this topic?
4. In Lines 66–67, Mary Ann states "I too have White guilt."
   a. How do other group members respond to her?
   b. What are some alternative ways that the group could have responded?
5. Where does this group miss opportunities to talk in dialogic ways?
6. In your opinion, how effective is this group at listening? What lines of talk or actions led you to this conclusion?
7. What deeper topic or message is Janice attempting to get Ted to "hear" in this excerpt?
8. Look at the speakers above. Choose one turn of talk for one speaker. Suggest a way that you could reframe his/her talk or actions to promote more dialogic conversation or repair conversation.

Excerpt 3

The conversation above in Excerpt 2 falters along as the speakers talk at each other to convince one another they are correct. For example, at one point Janice has a turn that is 17 lines long without interruption. (See Appendix C). Some speakers try to introduce topics that are not supported by others. For example, Janice and Mary Ann at different points attempt to introduce direct discussion of the term or idea "White guilt." Overall, there is very little listening taking place. Partly out of exasperation and in a demanding tone, Janice asks for an example (see Excerpt 3 below). Clearly, Janice is in a unique position in this conversation as the only group member who is biracial, and due to prior coursework and experience she was familiar with the term "White guilt"; her experience and prior knowledge no doubt contribute to her frustration. The exchange between Janice and Ted is followed by some turns where Mary Ann, in a measured, neutral tone, interacts with Ted:

135	*Ted:*	All I'm saying, bottom line all I was saying is I think she
136		[Walker-Dahlhouse] would make them use better mate-
137		rial, something that made them, instead of…
138	*Janice:*	Okay, give me an example. Give me an example, like…
139	*Ted:*	Um…
140	*Mary Ann:*	So you didn't like that they focused just on the African
141		Americans?
142	*Ted:*	No, what the whole unit, I'm not…it's more of a, a, how
143		do you put it? More of a conflicting story than one of
144		togetherness, a story of togetherness.
145	*Mary Ann:*	Oh, okay.
146	*Ted:*	You know a story where one party was oppressed, the
147		other one wasn't. Why couldn't they read a story that was
148		more, 'cause it was English class. It's not like it was a His-
149		tory class where they had to learn part A, or team A was
150		oppressive and…

151	*Mary Ann:*	So you would have rather have liked to have heard about
152		maybe um Harriet Tubman's journey and how the white
153		people helped her through that journey.
154	*Ted:*	Exactly.

Questions for Analysis Excerpt 3

1. While Ted is trying to think of an example, Mary Ann steps in to ask a question in Line 140. (Unlike Janice, her tone is not demanding or sarcastic; the question sounds authentic). How does her question help clarify what Ted is trying to say?
2. What do you notice about how Mary Ann responds to Ted's question in Line 144?
3. What conversational strategy does Mary Ann use in Line 149–151? How does this help Ted communicate his idea?
4. How might Mary Ann's responses to Ted in Lines 140, 144, and 149–151 be considered an example of Mary Ann attempting to play the believing game?
5. While Mary Ann helps Ted articulate his idea, how does his idea seem to go against what Mary Ann has wanted to discuss earlier (Lines 66–68)?
6. What conversational strategies could each speaker use to shift the conversation toward more dialogic talk?

Post-Analysis Procedures

1. If you can, compare your findings and analysis from the questions above with another group or pair of students. Look at specific examples cited in your analysis and compare them to the examples of another reader or other readers.
2. After you have completed #1 under post-analysis, consider the questions below. As you answer each question, cite evidence to support your assertions. Different members of your group may have different opinions, so try to be attentive to listening as well as speaking.

    a. Overall, how substantive or educational is the talk in this group? How do you know this?
    b. Can you think of a metaphor that would describe or typify this group interaction?
    c. What is your conclusion about how listening functions in this group?
    d. Revisit the definition of dialogic talk earlier in the chapter. Do you think this group is engaging in dialogic talk? Why or why not?
    e. What might you find to respect or admire in the ideas of this group or in the talk they use? What might you find disrespectful or less than admirable?
    f. What are some of the issues that this group is struggling with? (Consider both their talk interactions and the content they are addressing.)

g. Take the perspective of a group member. Brainstorm a list of things you could say or strategies that you could use to encourage a more dialogic process for listening and speaking. Think of how conversation can be repaired and reconstructed. It will be helpful to link your ideas specifically to lines of talk.

h. If you were a teacher listening to this group, what would you think about the type of dialogue being constructed? Why? If you were listening in on this conversation, what would you do next?

Concluding Thoughts on the Talk between Janice, Krissy, Mary Ann, and Ted

In looking across this conversation, we want to be clear that we personally do not endorse or agree with Ted's position that educators should only choose positive stories about history. Our own position is that we should not insulate children from the realities of differences based on race or our racialized histories, the inequities that have existed in our country, or the inequities that continue to exist. While the group is not successful in constructing a dialogic response to Ted, Janice is brave to name "White guilt" as the issue that has been raised (Lines 55–57). It is difficult to convey the risk that can be involved for a person of color to openly state such an issue with other speakers who are White.

We do applaud the fact that Ted was able to give voice to his concerns and share them out loud and that Mary Ann was willing to listen. As teacher educators, we recognize that in the excerpts above, Ted's talk identifies where he is as a learner. In contrast, he could merely parrot back what he had read, even though he did not agree with it or believe it. It is important that he shares his ideas honestly. We also admire Mary Ann for being able to suspend her own beliefs and opinions momentarily. Earlier in the conversation, Mary Ann attempted to pursue the discussion of "White guilt"—the term introduced by Janice, but Mary Ann was not able to gain the conversational floor around this topic. As the conversation unfolds, it becomes clear that Mary Ann did not agree with Ted. Near the end of this episode, Ted continues talking (continuing from Line 152):

Ted:	Exactly. Why couldn't they make it so nobody's the bad guy, everybody's the good guy type thing?
Janice:	(Overlapping with Ted) Well I got a question. By the same token . . .
Mary Ann:	But you have to teach both.
Ted:	That's reserved for history. This is English.

We see here that Mary Ann and Janice both respond, although Janice does not finish her question, which overlaps with Ted's talk. Mary Ann responds to Ted's question directly, and to Ted's assertion that African American literature should just show "everybody's the good guy." Mary Ann says, "But you have to teach both"—meaning that both perspectives must be represented—those that are positive and those that challenge us or that are painful or negative. This is also a reference back to the earlier conversation where Ted described presenting different perspectives during history lessons, particularly what he saw as perspectives that portrayed White people negatively.

As instructors, we are not satisfied with the listening in this group or with the way this group functioned as a whole on this night. There were several points that Mary Ann introduced, personal responses that were worthy of exploration in the group, but none of the group members responded with active listening. Even when Mary Ann attempted to discuss the notion of "White guilt," which was first voiced by Janice, no one, including Janice, responded in a way that demonstrated reflective listening. We recognize that Janice may have missed Mary Ann's willingness to take up the topic in part because of the potential risk to herself involved in introducing such a topic. However, based on the transcript on this night and others, a more likely interpretation is that Janice was trying to convince Ted that she was right—this was a common pattern in their talk. Unlike other scholars who have found that a single minority student is sometimes positioned as the representative of his/her race, we found no examples where group members positioned Janice in this way.

In these excerpts, Mary Ann is the only participant who responded by repeating what others had said, even if it meant shifting away from a point she had raised herself. This type of repetition demonstrates reflective listening and affords the potential to build conversational coherence, but it is also limiting because Ted, for example, does not reciprocate in ways that allow Mary Ann the conversational floor. Janice, on the other hand, in her talk and tone assumes a fairly combative stance, demanding an example, "Give me an example . . ." or stating that she has a question "Well, I gotta question . . .", but then preparing to make a statement as part of a larger argument, "By the same token . . ." In sum, neither Janice, Krissy, nor Ted demonstrate any type of believing game stance toward exploring Mary Ann's ideas. Repeatedly we see in this transcript that Mary Ann's attempts to engage more dialogically are unsupported by her group. On the other hand, because Mary Ann is trying to support others in their conversation, it means she does not have the opportunity to pursue topics that she begins to surface. Furthermore, in addition to the issue of White guilt, there is another challenging and deeper conversation that is not fully developed around the treatment of Native Americans as North America was colonized. While we do not delve into this topic here, this is also a possible discussion point that readers of this chapter can explore.

Conclusion

In this chapter, we have explored the important role of listening in dialogue. When members of a group talk *at* each other and not *with* one another, talk does not function dialogically. The limitations of dialogue in the examples here are co-constructed by all group members. Any one of these group members could have attempted to introduce conversational repairs or other conversational moves that would redirect conversation (e.g., see "Redirecting/Shifting Conversation" in Chapter 5, Appendix B). Although we do see some shifts in discourse, it is clear that the group struggles. While listening and conversational interactions are critically important, it should also be acknowledged that the group's topics, particularly those related to race and guilt, provide a major challenge. These topics are representative of what Glazier (2003) has called "hot lava"—they are topics that are too hot to touch and if one touches them, one is likely to get burned (p. 76). In Chapter 7, we discuss the issue of race and other hot lava topics in the context of multiple texts and perspectives.

References

Au, K.H. (1998). Social constructivism and the school literacy learning of students of diverse backgrounds. *Journal of Literacy Research, 30*(2), 297–319.

Burbules, N.C. (1993). *Dialogue in teaching: Theory and practice.* New York: Teachers College Press.

Delpit, L. (1988). The silenced dialogue: Power and pedagogy in educating other people's children. *Harvard Educational Review, 58*(3), 280–298.

Dewey, J. (1896). The reflex arc concept in psychology. *The Psychological Review, III*(4), 357–370.

Elbow, P. (2008). The believing game—Methodological believing. Retrieved from http:// works.bepress.com/peter_elbow/20

Glazier, J.A. (2003). Moving closer to speaking the unspeakable: White teachers talking about race. *Teacher Education Quarterly, 30*(1), 73–94.

Hankins, K. (2003). *Teaching through the storm.* New York: Teachers College Press.

Harris, V.J. (1992). African-American conceptions of literacy: A historical perspective. *Theory into Practice, 31*(4), 276–285.

Haroutunian-Gordon, S. (2010). Listening to a challenging perspective: The role of interruption. *Teachers College Record, 112*(11), 2793–2814.

McVee, M.B., Hopkins, M.B., & Bailey, N.M. (2011). Exploring culture as discursive process: Positioning in teacher explorations of literacy and diversity. In M.B. McVee, C.H. Brock, & J.A. Glazier (Eds.), *Sociocultural positioning in literacy: Exploring culture, discourse, narrative, and power in diverse educational contexts* (pp. 107–129). Cresskill, NJ: Hampton Press.

Parker, W. (2010). Listening to strangers: Classroom discussion in democratic education. *Teachers College Record, 112*(11), 2815–2832.

Rice, S., & Burbules, N.C. (2010). Listening: A virtue account. *Teachers College Record, 112*(11), 2728–2742.

Roy, D. (2011). The birth of a word. [Video File]. Retrieved from http://www.ted.com/ talks/deb_roy_the_birth_of_a_word

Rud, A.G., & Garrison, J. (2010). Reverence and listening in teaching and leading. *Teachers College Record, 112*(11), 2777–2792.

Shanahan, L.E., McVee, M.B., Schiller, J.A., Tynan, E.A., D'Abate, R.L., Flury-Kashmanian, C.M., . . . & Hayden, H.E. (2013). Supporting struggling readers and literacy clinicians through reflective video pedagogy. In E.T. Ortlieb & E.H. Cheek, Jr. (Eds.), *Advanced literacy practices: From the clinic to the classroom literacy* (Vol. 2). Bingley, UK: Emerald Group Publishing.

Walker-Dalhouse, D. (1992). Using African-American literature to increase ethnic understanding. *The Reading Teacher, 45*(6), 416–422.

Zarnowski, M. (1988). Learning about fictionalized biographies: A reading and writing approach. *The Reading Teacher, 42*(2), 136–141.

Transcript (Required Readings Read by Members of Discussion Group)

Au, K.H. (1998). Social constructivism and the school literacy learning of students of diverse backgrounds. *Journal of Literacy Research, 30*(2), 297–319.

Delpit, L. (1988). The silenced dialogue: Power and pedagogy in educating other people's children. *Harvard Educational Review, 58*(3), 280–298.

Transcript (Members of Discussion Group Chose Two of the Following)

Harris, V.J. (1992). African-American conceptions of literacy: A historical perspective. *Theory into Practice, 31*(4), 276–285.

Walker-Dalhouse, D. (1992). Using African-American literature to increase ethnic understanding. *The Reading Teacher, 45*(6), 416–422.

Zarnowski, M. (1988). Learning about fictionalized biographies: A reading and writing approach. *The Reading Teacher, 42*(2), 136–141.

Appendix A

Reverent Listening

Teachers wishing to engage in this type of dialogic discussion must also practice a particular type of listening: *reverent listening*. Rud and Garrison (2010) claim that teachers who demonstrate reverent listening enact the following stances and practices. Reverent teachers:

Demonstrate awe and wonder toward their subject matter. These teachers recognize that they are the experts in their classrooms with regard to subject matter, but continue to learn about their subject matter. Importantly, with regard to learners, these teachers are not "arrogant or presumptuous" (p. 2780).

Consider knowledge about subject matter and knowledge about students. These teachers listen carefully to their students. "[G]ood teachers must have the moral perception and imagination to connect to students, and the intellectual command of subject matter to readily reconfigure it" (p. 2780), and these teachers accept the risks that comes with such openness.

Model examples of the practices they teach. Teachers who practice reverent listening make connections and model for their students. This process of modeling and connection is grounded in listening. "One cannot connect and model until he or she has listened and learned about what others need, desire, and dream" (p. 2781).

Give respect. These teachers listen to and treat students with respect and expect a community based on mutual respect. These "teachers seek to share their values of self-transcending care, concern, and compassion" (p. 2781).

Value ritual and ceremony. These structures help us to structure, organize, and manage classroom life, but also to create spaces to listen and also create spaces for all students to have a voice. While ritual and ceremony are created, in part, through repetition, reverent teaching also recognizes that "In a good community, one's place is not fixed; it is dynamic and alters as the needs of the community may require" (p. 2783).

Practice silence and humility. These teachers do not use their knowledge or power for authoritarian purposes or expressions of arrogance. While such teachers are actively engaged in listening to learners, they also listen for silences and attempt to create openings particularly for those students who "might otherwise maintain a subjugated silence" (p. 2784). In their own expressions of knowledge, these teachers are also comfortable acknowledging their own limits if they do not know the particular answer to a question.

Appendix B

Abstracts of Articles Read for Class

Required Readings Read by Members of Discussion Group

Au, K.H. (1998). Social constructivism and the school literacy learning of students of diverse backgrounds. *Journal of Literacy Research, 30*(2), 297–319.

Abstract. Part of a special issue on multicultural issues in literacy research and practice. There is growing concern about the gap between the school literacy achievement of students of diverse backgrounds and those of mainstream backgrounds. The most plausible explanations for this gap from a social constructivist stance are linguistic differences, cultural differences, discrimination, inferior education, and rationales for schooling. A conceptual framework for addressing the literacy achievement gap is proposed.

Delpit, L. (1988). The silenced dialogue: Power and pedagogy in educating other people's children. *Harvard Educational Review, 58*(3), 280–298.

Abstract. Lisa Delpit uses the debate over process-oriented versus skills-oriented writing instruction as the starting-off point to examine the "culture of power" that exists in society in general and in the educational environment in particular. She analyzes five complex rules of power that explicitly and implicitly influence the debate over meeting the educational needs of Black and poor students on all levels. Delpit concludes that teachers must teach all students the explicit and implicit rules of power as a first step toward a more just society.

Each Member of the Discussion Group Chose Two of the Following

Harris, V.J. (1992). African-American conceptions of literacy: A historical perspective. *Theory into Practice, 31*(4), 276–285.

Abstract. Examines conceptions of literacy held by African Americans by reviewing written works produced by the ethnic minority. Interchangeability of literacy with education and schooling; Attainment of literacy as a way of participating in all cultural institutions; Access to and the philosophy of literacy; Division of the conceptual history of Black literacy into five periods.

Walker-Dalhouse, D. (1992). Using African-American literature to increase ethnic understanding. *The Reading Teacher, 45*(6), 416–422.

Abstract. Tells the story of how the author used literature in an attempt to extend her students' multicultural knowledge of African-American culture. Shares information about her background, her beliefs about literacy, the students she taught, and the setting for her literature lessons. Article lists books used; Also used literature-based Houghton Mifflin Reading Program; Why valuing parallel cultures is important.

Zarnowski, M. (1988). Learning about fictionalized biographies: A reading and writing approach. *The Reading Teacher, 42*(2), 136–141.

Abstract. This project promotes the learning of reading skills and content information at the same time, especially for low-ability readers and 4th-grade students. Describes procedures and planning steps used by the author for reading and writing in content areas to construct a fictionalized biography.

Appendix C

Complete Transcript Excerpt

Janice, Krissy, Mary Ann, and Ted: A Group Discussion

1	*Mary Ann:*	We're supposed to focus on Delpit and Au.
2	*Ted:*	Oh, good then you won't mind if I hated it.
3	*Janice:*	I wrote 'Delpit and all' because it was you know…
4	*Ted:*	Required.
5	*Mary Ann:*	Which one did you hate?
6	*Janice:*	See I was gonna find a nice way to say that.
7	*Ted:*	The one that you loved [Walker-Dahlhouse].
8	*Mary Ann:*	The one that I loved? Why?
9	*Ted:*	It brought back some memories and…
10	*Mary Ann:*	Of what?
11	*Janice:*	What, what did it bring…?
12	*Mary Ann:*	Oh my gosh. I even said that this article gives me pride as
13		being a teacher and you're probably like: What?! There's
14		pride in you? It was all about-oh-what's her name?

15		Walker-Dahlhouse went into a school and pretty much
16		said, brought in African American culture. She brought in
17		African American culture kind of unit to like to teach the
18		students and hoping that they will take away this knowl-
19		edge and continue wanting to know more about different
20		culture and I really liked it because…
21	*Krissy:*	(interrupting) So we're supposed to feel guilty because the white
22		male gets more money than them?
23	*Mary Ann:*	Oh, it's a male thing. Oh, okay.
24	*Ted:*	It's a white…(trails off)
25	*Janice:*	Okay I'm just listening.
26	*Krissy:*	No, because that is. The, there's like, like for example, I
27		know this one lady, she's in the high percentage who was
28		like in the highly paying women in the entire country,
29		she was in that small percentage up there, but it's even,
30		they say…(trails off)
31	*Mary Ann:*	Help me, help me. Where are we?
32	*Janice:*	What page are you on?
33	*Ted:*	I'm not on any page. I'm just talking in general.
34	*Mary Ann:*	"Using African literature to increase…" (reading from
35		Walker-Dahlhouse title)
36	*Ted:*	Get out of there. You're doing more harm than good.
37		("You" is unclear here.)
38		(Speakers are often overlapping for the next few exchanges)
39	*Mary Ann:*	No, I wanna know why…
40	*Krissy:*	No, I'm trying to understand.
41	*Janice:*	Ted, I swear to God, all I'm going to do is listen. I
42		swear…to God.
43	*Ted:*	Okay, what happened was, now what happened was
44		when I was student teaching, I taught on the Iroquois
45		Indian. What you're talking, you learn about the Native
46		Americans is…
47	*Janice:*	That's cool.
48	*Mary Ann:*	They play Lacrosse.
49	*Ted:*	…is that the white man throughout the book brought
50		smallpox and…
51	*Mary Ann:*	We killed them out.
52	*Ted:*	We killed them. We burned their buildings. We raped
53		their women.
54	*Mary Ann:*	We were horrible.
55	*Ted:*	We stole their land.
56	*Mary Ann:*	We did though.
57	*Ted:*	And one kid comes up to me and he's like, "Did we ever
58		do anything right?" like sarcastically and it's like, it reminded
59		me of this because it's like a guilt trip, like you're bad…

60	*Janice:*	No, that's what it's called, I swear to God and I'm not
61		making this up. I am not making this up, it's gonna sound
62		like I am, but there is actually like, in my other class I
63		have this entire book, I swear to God and it goes both
64		ways. It goes like on both, um, a first impression. What
65		you're feeling right now is called
66	*Mary Ann:*	Survivor's guilt.
67	*Janice:*	um, white guilt. I swear to God, it's called white guilt.
68	*Krissy:*	Well, yeah.
69	*Ted:*	I wrote that down. It's like…
70	*Janice:*	No, it's literally called "white guilt." There is, I swear.
71	*Mary Ann:*	But you know what? I too have white guilt especially
72		when I thought about how I wrote this piece on how,
73		oh, when I went to school back in the eighties…
74	*Ted:*	…what about self-esteem, you know, something like that.
75		I mean I'm not a big fan of teaching self-esteem in the
76		classroom but…
77	*Krissy:*	Oh, meaning, meaning like they read these stories…
78	*Ted:*	But I mean they should at least not feel bad, you know, at
79		least go home and say I don't care, my parents were jerks.
80	*Mary Ann:*	Well you know what I call that? I call that the hidden
81		curriculum.
82	*Janice:*	But your parents…I feel bad when people, go ahead.
83	*Krissy:*	You know what part of it is? Part of it is, is, it's like, it's
84		almost like you're guilty for what your ancestors or what
85		your fathers did.
86	*Mary Ann:*	Guilt by association.
87	*Krissy:*	In a way. In a sense.
88	*Janice:*	Can I make a suggestion please?
89	*Ted:*	Please do.
90	*Janice:*	Honestly, okay. Because believe it or not, I actually like
91		have many friends and we've had this conversation, like
92		serious conversation. You know, how can I say this? You
93		gotta think about the press, okay? All of the you know
94		bad, oppressive white people. They're the ones who got
95		the press, okay? And they got the press because, I mean it
96		happened and it needed to be said and it needed to be you
97		know put out there, but you know at the same time, there
98		were white people stompin' on the necks of other people
99		and I'm not just gonna go for the black heart, I'm gonna
100		go for everybody 'cause the Native Americans got hit the
101		hardest, and I think they're still getting hit the hardest, but
102		at the same time there were white people stompin' on the
103		necks of people of color, there were also white people
104		telling them, 'Stop that shit.' Okay, there were also white

105		people telling 'em, you know, while we were out there
106		marching and there were Klan members, there were also
107		white people marching with us, so it's who you choose
108		to align yourself with. If you do the whole white guilt
109		thing…
110	*Krissy:*	Don't take it so personally.
111	*Janice:*	…that's natural, but don't, don't…
112	*Ted:*	See, but that's the thing. I don't have white guilt. Does
113		that make me a bad person?
114	*Mary Ann:*	No.
115	*Ted:*	I mean her (unclear who "her" refers to) ancestors have
116		been here longer than my ancestors. My ancestors have
117		been here less than 50 years. Did I, was I responsible for
118		anything that was…that bad, like…
119	*Janice:*	Well, I think at the same time though, if you don't…
120	*Ted:*	Or should I feel guilty for what other people did? I mean
121		do I feel guilty about what the, you know, Huns did?
122	*Mary Ann:*	You can't ignore it. You have to accept it and I think,
123		and just go on. I mean that's not, it's a very general, easy
124		way…
125	*Ted:*	But I also felt, wouldn't it be more relevant to teach them
126		about their own culture since their culture's diverse in
127		their own neighborhood? I mean they had Hispanic and
128		Vietnamese and…why didn't they learn about, I know
129		they tried to, but it was…You're an English teacher and
130		you know the differences between the different kinds of
131		literature, you know, multicultural literature, but when
132		you read a History textbook, it's totally different.
133	*Mary Ann:*	Because it loses a voice.
134	*Ted:*	It's just…black, white, Native American. It's just this is
135		what happened. It's like there's no…
136	*Mary Ann:*	It loses a personal voice. It loses that connection, that per-
137		sonal feeling in it. This is, yeah, this is the right or wrong way.
138	*Ted:*	Janice was saying, you know, there are some, it's who you
139		align yourself with and it's team A and team B and team
140		A did this to team B and team B's upset and it's…
141	*Janice:*	But what if, I mean, you know, the ugly reality is, it did
142		happen and it did happen a lot for a long time, still hap-
143		pening and mostly by people who look like you [white
144		and male]. Mean it, love you, love you, mean it, love you,
145		mean it, love you, mean it, but…but at the same time, I
146		mean…I guess the, I guess, what are you gonna do with it?
147	*Ted:*	All I'm saying, bottom line all I was saying is I think she
148		[Walker-Dahlhouse] would make them use better mate-
149		rial, something that made them, instead of…

150	*Janice:*	Okay, give me an example. Give me an example, like…
151	*Ted:*	Um…
152	*Mary Ann:*	So you didn't like that they focused just on the African
153		Americans?
154	*Ted:*	No, what the whole unit, I'm not…it's more of a, a, how
155		do you put it? More of a conflicting story than one of
156		togetherness, a story of togetherness.
157	*Mary Ann:*	Oh, okay.
158	*Ted:*	You know a story where one party was oppressed, the
159		other one wasn't. Why couldn't they read a story that was
160		more, 'cause it was English class. It's not like it was a His-
161		tory class where they had to learn part A, or team A was
162		oppressive and…
163	*Mary Ann:*	So you would have rather have liked to have heard about
164		maybe um Harriet Tubman's journey and how the white
165		people helped her through that journey.
166	*Ted:*	Exactly. Why couldn't they make it so nobody's the bad
167		guy, everybody's the good guy type thing?
168	*Janice:*	Well I got a question. By the same token…
169	*Mary Ann:*	But you have to teach both.
170	*Ted:*	That's reserved for History. This is English.

7

EXPLORING HOT LAVA

Using Multiple Texts to Reflect on Multiple Positions Around Challenging Topics

Children familiar with the game "Hot Lava" know that as soon as someone yells "hot lava!" any space becomes an obstacle course. If hot lava is invoked, every participant has to navigate around the lava without getting burned. If children are playing at home, this might mean hopping from couch to chair to floor pillow to the dog bed without touching the floor. If kids are on the playground, it might mean avoiding all the wood chips and staying only on the playground equipment. Stepping off the safe zones and onto the lava means being burned and losing the game. In this chapter, we use the metaphor of hot lava to talk about the response that some of us may have to issues that we may not be comfortable discussing.

REFLECTION QUESTIONS

Consider the comments below. Each one surfaces a topic that could be considered hot lava. We use the word "could" intentionally because we recognize that what is hot lava for one person may not be hot lava for another.

1. What topic(s) do speakers refer to that could be considered hot lava?
2. Which of these topics would you designate as hot lava? Why?
3. How does each speaker position herself/himself or others?
4. Write a response to one of the speakers. Try to take the position of an empathetic listener. What would it mean to play the believing game here? What beliefs would you have to accept? How comfortable are you accepting those beliefs?
5. How would others in your social circle view the comments below? How would your social circles respond to these speakers?
6. Are there any topics expressed below that you do not feel are hot lava? Why?

---

1) Becky is a White, English-speaking teacher who was raised in a middle-class suburban community. She is teaching in an urban school with a predominantly African American student population. In discussing the use of running records to assess a child's reading development, Becky makes this comment: "I know they say that you aren't supposed to mark the kids down for issues of pronunciation or dialect. I mean, Dr. Johnston told us that, so I know that I'm not supposed to do that. But it's just that their English is so bad, and it's wrong if they say "axe" instead of "ask." They read it wrong. It's wrong. I'm gonna mark it wrong."

2) Jennifer, an African American student, comments during class as she critiques Shirley Brice Heath's study *Ways with Words,* a study of working-class and middle-class White and African American communities in the rural Piedmont Carolinas: "I grew up in a home where both my parents are professionals—I grew up in the suburbs in California—but my grandmother told us lots of stories about her growing up in the South. When she was [a] kid, they were very poor, and she said they went to bed hungry a lot. Even though we had what we needed, I know what it's like to be poor because she told us. I don't think Heath could understand that; she was a White person going into a community to look at literacy and to study an African American community. I have more in common with the Black people in Heath's book than Heath did because we're all Black. We all share more in common because of our race. That matters more than where you grow up."

3) James, a White student who grew up in extreme poverty, writes: "I don't understand why everyone is always making such a big deal of what race they are or what language they speak. I grew up poor—White and poor—in a city known for its population of poor, Black kids, drug problems, and gangs. Sometimes I was the only White kid in my classes and there were only a few of us in the whole school. But you know what, I worked hard. I graduated and put myself through school. Why can't people just suck it up? Race doesn't matter. Being poor doesn't matter. Hard work does."

4) Reggie, an African American male student who attended a school in a suburban area, commented: "Well, for a lot of Black students like myself, we just see school as acting White. I grew up in the suburbs, but I didn't fit in. Everyone was White, and I mean EV-ER-Y-ONE. There weren't that many kids who weren't White, Brown kids or Black kids or kids who didn't speak English, and we hung out, but I didn't do school. Doing school like taking classes like Chemistry, A.P. English Literature and all that, that's just acting White."

5) Bethany, a White woman, talks about her student teaching placement in a rural agrarian community. "I grew up in the 'burbs, so I had never seen anything like it. The kids all skipped school on the first day of hunting season. They even had a 'drive your tractor to school day.' I am not kidding, it was like total rednecks-ville! Then, in addition to the rednecks, there were the migrant families. I felt so sorry for those kids. They would show up for a few weeks because their parents hauled them around the country to find work. They could barely speak English and the parents would never come to school and you couldn't call them or contact

them unless you went to go find them because there were no phone numbers or addresses. It's sad because they just didn't care about their kids' education."

6) Maria, a bilingual English- and Spanish-speaking student who was raised in the US in a middle-class home with Mexican immigrant parents, relayed this story: "Isaac's mother came to see me. I know she means well because she's trying so hard, but she's got three kids and works nights. Dad's not in the picture. Isaac is so reluctant to read, but Mom said he spends lots of time playing Mario Cart and he has these crazy books he puts together where he writes stories and draws pictures about the game. She even suggested that maybe we could use the video game as a way to get him interested in reading. OK, let's stop right there. The video game is the reason the kid can't read—he spends his time playing video games. That's the whole problem! No, we are not gonna use the video game to help him learn to read. You need to get your child some books and read to him like my parents did."

wrong approach

7) Bernie, a White male, writes: "I don't think we need to learn about issues related to gays and lesbians. This is a private matter related to people's personal choice. If someone chooses to be gay, that's their issue. When we read about the teacher who said 'That's right' to the girl who said, 'Boys don't kiss boys,' I don't see what the big deal is. Teachers shouldn't have to deal with this. It's personal, like religion, and it doesn't have anything to do with literacy anyway."

So . . . you're a _____! Me too!

In response the vignettes above, we make a bold statement. None of us, regardless of race, ethnicity, language, gender, economic status, or cultural heritage, is free from bias or prejudice. In the vignettes above, we see that individuals of all backgrounds can hold stereotypes or biases that shape their interpretation. These interpretations can become "single stories" that influence teacher's thoughts and views about children and learning. None of us are immune from the ways in which our own culture, identity, and experiences lead us to interpret the world and those who we encounter in it. We are all, at one point or another, racist or classist or bigoted or homophobic or. . . . This is not an excuse, but a recognition that we all have something yet to learn. Some of us might have more experience than others, but if we listen reflectively, we can learn from one another, even as we challenge one another. Further, we can learn to challenge ourselves.

Talking about challenging issues such as race, class, gender, religion, or sexual orientation can be a lot like dealing with hot lava—it's a good way to get burned! Some of us may have even been taught that it was not polite to talk about these issues. On the other hand, some of us may have been taught to be on the defensive and to begin verbal combat whenever anything suggests bias or prejudice.

In the remainder of this chapter, we return to the conversation between Mary Ann, Ted, Janice, and Krissy to more deeply explore how their talk crosses into or avoids hot lava, in particular, around the issue of race. We then examine academic writing from two students around a particular text and ask what we can learn from the students' close reading and academic reflective writing. We close the chapter with further examples of students reflecting on and through multimodal compositions to explore challenging, but important, topics. We ask that you keep in mind the definitions of reflection and dialogue introduced in Chapter 6:

Reflection is:

a goal-directed process that moves teachers to identify a situation, process, or experience that is puzzling, interesting, celebratory, or otherwise intriguing and view it through multiple lenses. Developing particular skill sets or dispositions is necessary for reflection, but a particular set of skills or dispositions is not sufficient to become a reflective practitioner. Reflective teachers strive to gain strategic knowledge of a situation in order to develop and explore questions, recognize, or acknowledge complexity of situations, processes or experiences, and make adaptations to their actions, beliefs, positions, and classroom and pedagogical practices. Reflection is interpretive in that individuals bring their knowledge and experiences to the situation. Reflection is self-directed and collaborative in nature.

(Shanahan et al., 2013, p. 305)

Dialogue is:

an activity directed toward discovery and new understanding, which stands to improve the knowledge, insight, or sensitivity of its participants. . . . Dialogue represents a continuous, developmental communicative interchange through which we stand to gain a fuller apprehension of the world, ourselves, and one another.

(Burbules, 1993, p. 8)

Keeping these definitions in mind, we return to the conversation of Ted, Krissy, Janice, and Mary Ann.

Reflection and Dialogue in Book Club: A Look at Hot Lava

At one point when sharing the complete transcript of the conversation between Krissy, Janice, Mary Ann, and Ted from the last chapter (Appendix C) with students, one student turned to the course instructor Mary and asked, "Oh my gosh, are we all this dysfunctional?" In reading the entire transcript, it becomes apparent that there are tensions in this group. But we remind readers that the point of this exercise is not to point out any group's supposed "dysfunction." The point is to observe the places where talk falls apart or gets too hot to handle. In observing one group, on one particular night, we are only seeing a small glimpse of the group's interactions, and the only way to fully judge a student's overall learning in the class would be to examine all of their work: talk, writing, multimodal composing, Book Logs, and other assignments. Furthermore, despite the limitations on talk in the group, they do manage to give voice to some challenging topics. In contrast, other groups may avoid these topics altogether and maintain what McIntyre (1997) has called "a culture of niceness" (p. 40). We have often seen a culture of niceness in our own classes where students fear risking upsetting others and maintain talk about surface issues or relatively safe topics. Such a culture can be just as limiting as a combative classroom culture.

Readers may recall that talk on this night got off to a rocky start with multiple speakers vying for the conversational floor and real confusion about what the conversation was about. Mary Ann directly voiced this confusion when she said: "Help me, help me. Where are we?" This early part of the conversation is disjointed with a lot of overlapping talk and a lack of coherence. There are indications early on of a conflict between Ted and Janice. In Line 23, Ted begins: "It's a White . . ." but trails off before completing his thought, and Janice follows this with, "Okay, I'm listening." The incoherent conversation preceding and following seem to indicate that Janice, and perhaps others, were not listening as well. Only a short time later (Line 39), Janice interjects: "Ted, I swear to God, all I'm going to do is listen. I swear . . . to God." Ted then begins his story of experiences when he was student teaching in a history classroom. Notice the conversational coherence that seems to build between Ted and Mary Ann.

45	*Ted:*	[What you learn about Native Americans] is that the white
46		man throughout the book brought smallpox and
47	*Mary Ann:*	We killed them out.
48	*Ted:*	We killed them. We burned their buildings. We raped their
49		women.
50	*Mary Ann:*	We were horrible.
51	*Ted:*	We stole their land.
52	*Mary Ann:*	We did though.
53	*Ted:*	And one kid comes up to me and he's like, "Did we ever do
54		anything right?" like sarcastically and it's like, it reminded
55		me of this because it's like a guilt trip, like you're bad
56	*Janice:*	No, that's what it's called, I swear to God and I'm not mak-
57		ing this up. I am not making this up, it's gonna sound like
58		I am, but there is actually like, in my other class I have this
59		entire book, I swear to God and it goes both ways. It goes
60		like on both, um, a first impression. What you're feeling
61		right now is called
62	*Mary Ann:*	Survivor's guilt.
63	*Janice:*	um, white guilt. I swear to God, it's called white guilt.
64	*Krissy:*	Well, yeah.
65	*Ted:*	I wrote that down. It's like
66	*Janice:*	No, it's literally called "white guilt." There is, I swear.
67	*Mary Ann:*	But you know what? I too have white guilt

Interestingly, what seems to be conversational coherence is actually Ted building up a particular storyline—"We mistreated Native Americans"—for the purpose of calling it into question. Essentially, his point in the longer excerpt is that his family only arrived in the US during the last 50 years, so they weren't responsible for any of these past wrongs. Ted equates the "negative" stories of the past with a "guilt trip." At this point, Janice can no longer sustain her promise to listen, and she says what Ted is feeling is "White guilt." Janice is correct in her assertion that White guilt is the label often applied to the feelings of guilt that Ted describes. At this point, Mary Ann admits, "I too have White guilt."

Seldom do students speak as frankly as Mary Ann when she says, "I too have White guilt." This seems like a pivotal connection point. Janice is trying to introduce a new term. Ted is trying to introduce an idea, and Mary Ann uses the term "White guilt" and admits to having similar feelings. It is not difficult to imagine a different scene altogether where the group directly tackles the difficult topic in a dialogic manner.

Mary Ann:	I too have White guilt.
Janice:	I'm curious about that. What does 'White guilt' mean to you? Is there an example?
Ted:	How about my example—the student feeling bad about what he learned in history? That seems like White guilt because he's feeling guilty about the bad stuff because he's White and it was all done by White people. I don't know if he would feel that way if he wasn't White, would he? But, I'd like to know more what you guys think.
Krissy *(to Mary Ann):*	You have your computer here—can you search White guilt? I'm curious what it will say. Maybe that will help us. Let's look at a definition.
Janice:	Even before we do that I'd be interested in what all of us *think* it is. How 'bout if we just take a minute to jot down our ideas on a piece of paper? Then we could look at differences and similarities.

However, this imagined connection point and possible conversation never surfaced. Mary Ann's remarkable admission and the possible connection point pass quickly, as both Ted and Janice try to maintain the floor—Ted to complete his bigger storyline and Janice to try to rebut what Ted is saying. In Line 80, Janice asks if she can make a suggestion, to which Ted responds positively, but sarcastically, "Please do." Janice then takes an extended turn (17 lines). During this turn of talk, she does not make a suggestion, but attempts to help educate Ted about White guilt.

There are some unusual markers in this conversation. First, when Ted begins talking about how students feel guilty, Janice actually introduces the term "White guilt." On top of that, it is unusual that Mary Ann attempts to discuss this openly, where in Line 66 she says, "But you know what? I too have White guilt . . ." There is long-standing research that has documented how White teachers avoid exactly this type of conversation related to race (cf. Frankenberg, 1993; McIntyre, 1997; McVee, Baldassarre, & Bailey, 2004). Although they are not successful, Mary Ann and Janice at different times try to introduce race into the conversation; that difficult conversation is not sustained. It is clear that the topics of race and White guilt are both difficult to contend with and participants veer away from these, avoiding the conversational "hot lava" that could potentially burn them.

Part of the challenge facing the group are those biases that never quite come to the surface, or what Joyce King (1991) would call **"dysconscious racism."** King writes:

> Dysconsciousness is an uncritical habit of mind (including perceptions, attitudes, assumptions, and beliefs) that justifies inequity and exploration by accepting the existing order of things as given. . . . Dysconscious racism is a form of racism that tacitly accepts dominant White norms and privileges. It is not the absence of consciousness . . . but an impaired consciousness or distorted way of thinking. (p. 133)

One example of dysconscious racism is built into Ted's assertion that history is just facts and that there is no voice; minorities have long argued that the dominant voice, or White, male voice, in particular, is the one that gets to narrate history. Also, Ted's assertion that the realistic stories are for History and not for English reflects a concrete boundary around disciplinary knowledge arguing that some topics, particularly negative ones, do not belong in school settings.

Position, Reflection and Dialogue in Academic Writing: Janice and Karen Write about the "Culture of Power"

In the beginning of this chapter, we have provided a close examination of dialogue in face-to-face talk. But in Book Logs or other reflective responses, traditional academic writing is still important. In this section, we introduce you to a contrastive analysis of two excerpts from the writing from Janice and Karen in response to Lisa Delpit's (1988) "The Silenced Dialogue." Although Delpit's original article is somewhat dated since the literacy field is no longer debating whole language vs. phonics, even the original article is still highly relevant to today's school environment and considerations of student learning. Among other ideas, Delpit argued that some children need to be taught the "culture of power" explicitly in order to succeed in school and in society—this includes explicit instruction in certain aspects of literacy. Part of Delpit's premise is that those who are part of mainstream culture and society often learn the rules of power tacitly because they are surrounded by and operate within these rules as part of everyday life. These rules are part of their family and community culture. In contrast, Delpit asserts that many minorities are kept from knowing these rules because they, or their families, are not part of the "culture of power."

Even though Delpit's article was published first in 1988, students still need to learn about cultures of power, particularly if they are outside the mainstream. Recent events in education, and in society at large, demonstrate that there are still strong divisions along racial lines in the United States and other countries, and teachers are not exempt from these divisions or from the "silenced dialogue." In Delpit's original article, Black teachers who were tired of trying to state their beliefs merely stopped talking (i.e., the "silenced dialogue"), and their lack of talk was viewed as agreement.

QUESTIONS FOR ANALYSIS. AS YOU READ THROUGH THE TWO EXCERPTS BELOW (JANICE AND KAREN) CONSIDER THESE QUESTIONS:

1. What do you notice about the content of each excerpt?
2. What do you notice about how the writer positions herself?
3. How does the writer make use of multiple texts (e.g., academic articles, memoir or autobiography, narratives, her own life texts)?
4. What do you notice about the writing style in each excerpt? (Look at the organization, structure, sentence style, use of APA citations, etc.)
5. What purpose do you think the writing served for the writer?

In the excerpts below, both Janice and Karen discuss the fifth or final rule of power that Delpit introduces in her article.

Janice's Excerpt of Academic Writing about Delpit

[Rule] 5. Those with power are frequently least aware of its existence. . . . Those with less power are often more aware. . . . When one is a member of the COP [Culture of Power], one does not feel it because it's taken for granted, it's enmeshed into their environment and understood. When one is not a member of the COP, one feels that too. One notices the disparity in different aspects of their life; one notices the under-representation of themselves. One feels the difference.

Delpit says that parents who do not function inside that COP want something more for their children, "They want to ensure that the school provides their children with discourse patterns, interactional styles, and spoken and written language codes that will allow them success in a larger society." P.285

These parents want their children to at least have a shot at being members of the Culture of Power.

Karen's Excerpt of Academic Writing about Delpit

The final rule of power was the portion of this article that caused the most enlightenment for me. It states: "Those with power are frequently least aware of—or least willing to acknowledge its existence. Those with less power are often the most aware of its existence" (Delpit, 1988, p. 283). This was an uncomfortable topic for me to examine since I am a member of the so-called "culture of power" due to my economic class. The thought of exhibiting cultural power over my minority students was something I chose not to think about. Yet through my vignettes and other readings this semester, I have begun to unfold some of the unconscious feelings of superiority over certain groups. I know that this sounds terrible coming from a person that educates children, but I am only telling of my prejudices as part of the learning process. The statement: "I want the same thing for everyone else's children as I want for my own" sparked a response that I had never expected. I now realize that I want the same thing for everyone else's children as long as it meets the standards and values of my White middle class culture. I began to think of how I would feel if schools began to reflect the African American culture to meet the needs and values of their students. I now confirm my unconscious feelings of superiority. I began to immediately worry about placing my child in a school of this culture because I felt that it lowered the standards for my child. Au argues against these feelings from a social constructivist point of view as she labels it discrimination: "The argument is that American society and its system of schooling are structured to prevent equality of educational opportunity and outcome" (Au, 1998, p. 302). Delpit takes my thoughts even further as she brings forth the idea that we can make ourselves believe that we are operating out of good intentions but may have unconscious motives (Delpit, 1988, p. 285).

We can summarize some of the major differences across the excerpts in Table 7.1. We have added in some facts from a comparison of the entire written responses.

The table shows that Karen's excerpt and her complete written reflection are about twice as long as Janice's writing. But, as any writing teacher can tell you, it is not the quantity of the writing that matters but the quality. What is clear in the excerpts, and even more so in the extended writing, is the depth of reflection present in Karen's work. What do we mean by "depth of reflection?"

Karen does not just summarize or paraphrase Delpit. She goes beyond restating Delpit's ideas. For example, in the excerpt she makes the initial quote work for her, using it as a platform to build ideas upon. Karen's ideas do not merely

TABLE 7.1 Comparison of writing by Janice and Karen

EXCERPT	Janice	Karen
# of words	145	336
Content	Restate Delpit's 5th rule in the culture of power. Summarize the article.	Restate Delpit's 5th rule in the culture of power. Explore her response to this rule.
Self-positioning	Uses impersonal pronouns (e.g., "one"). Makes no reference or connection to self in writing.	Uses personal pronouns (e.g., "I"). Makes connections between the reading and self. Considers her own position(s).
Multiple texts	Makes connection to Delpit.	Makes specific connection to Delpit and Au. Specifically mentions her feelings based on experience. Generally references her life text (vignettes) and "other readings."
Writing Style	Summary, paraphrase, quote. Little evidence used for supporting ideas. Tries to follow APA.	Summary, paraphrase, quotes, personal response. Evidence to support and develop ideas. Examples. Follows APA.

ENTIRE WRITTEN RESPONSE

# of words	948	2063
Purpose of writing	Complete an assignment.	Explore, examine, respond.
References	6	6
Degree of intertextual positioning within writing	Low	High

summarize more of Delpit's thinking, but her ideas connect to her own personal responses and thoughts. Karen shares these personal feelings (e.g., This was an uncomfortable topic . . .), but she does not stop by merely stating feelings. She explores those feelings, connecting them to other thoughts about inequity in schooling, and she provides evidence from other texts (e.g., the quote from Kathy Au) to develop and support her point. In our analysis, she maintains a high degree of intertextual positioning within the writing. She connects across multiple texts, looping back to self, and then connecting again to other texts to consider others' perspectives. Karen's response also lays bare some harsh truths as she acknowledges some "prejudices." Karen seems aware that she is taking a risk when she acknowledges these prejudices; she states that "I know that this sounds terrible coming from a person that educates children . . ." In sum, Karen has engaged in deep reflection and dialogue that aligns well with the definitions by Shanahan, et al. (2013) and Burbules (1993).

In contrast to Karen, Janice plays it safe in her writing. Unlike the exploratory and well-connected writing that Karen develops, Janice stays with paraphrase and summary. Her purpose seems to be just completing an assignment. Not only does she not make any personal connections to the text, she further distances herself by using generic pronouns such as "When one is not a member of the COP, one feels that too." Perhaps most striking is the fact that Janice does not make a single connection to the text that is reflexive, that speaks to her beliefs or feelings about the text, or that connects to her own experience. This is particularly striking because at one point in her Book Club group, she had asserted: "I'm really, really, super-duper, super, super, super, super well-informed about Lisa Delpit's writing."

Dialogue Through Other Means: Narrative and Multimodal Composition

The example of talk that opens this chapter is situated within a face-to-face book club discussion. But, frameworks for dialogue and the seeds of reflection are often planted as students articulate their thoughts in Book Logs or narrative writing. We conclude this chapter by sharing some examples of students engaging in dialogue with others and themselves as they develop narrative writing or multimodal compositions.

David's Story

In response to the narrative vignette about a border-crossing experience (see Chapter 2), David, a White male, chose coming out as a gay man for his border-crossing experience. David narrated this story in several ways. He wrote linguistic text to track his ideas (see McVee, Fronczak, Stainsby, & White, 2015, pp. 66–68). Moreover, he used various multimodal compositions combined with text; one of his revisions of the vignette was a visual interpretation that combined linguistic text, shape, and color (see Figure 7.1). This represented a prison of negative terms, such as "Queer," "Failure," "It's a phase," "R U Gay?" and "Homophobia." Below this representation, David listed positive words in a rainbow pattern reminiscent of the flag that has come to represent the LGBTQ (Lesbian, Gay, Bisexual, Transgender, and Queer) movement and tolerance. Each positive attribute was linked to one of the rainbow colors: ACCEPTANCE (red), TRUTH (orange), SELF WORTH (yellow), HAPPINESS (green), PEACE (blue), LOVE (Violet), and HOPE (Lavender).

In reflecting upon his experiences of sharing his ideas with others, David wrote:

> . . . in the past I had only explored this topic through a linguistic mode, but this project called for students to respond using multiple modes, intentionally

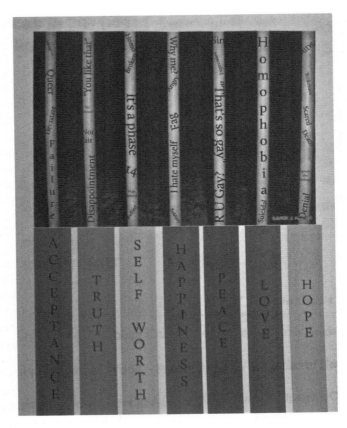

FIGURE 7.1 David's multimodal representation of his border-crossing experience. (View in color at marymcvee.com.)

layering semiotic signs to communicate meaning through three multimodal representations of our border crossing. Through each representation, I was pushing myself to more deeply reflect and unpack my border crossing. My life became the text that I was responding to authentically.

But it was not just me who had the opportunity to respond, it was also my peers. It was through my experience in these small groups that I came to appreciate the diverse backgrounds of each individual in the class.

(McVee et al., 2015, p. 67)

David's point here is a profound one. As David had opportunity to talk and share about himself, he was not only exploring his own story in a new way, he was learning the stories and diverse backgrounds of others. It is worth noting that "diverse" backgrounds were with a group of individuals who at first may not have appeared diverse. The students in David's discussion group identified as White students, but they realized that although they were White and attending the same university, in addition to race and gender differences, they had many other unique experiences and types of diversity to celebrate.

> As teachers, we have the privilege of spending an extensive period of time with students. It is our responsibility to notice our students, appreciate them, and celebrate their differences. As with reflection, this noticing takes time, a precious and limited resource in schools. Even if we do not have the time to confer individually with each child each day, teachers can communicate the daily message that we do not view differences as deficits. As teachers we can take genuine interest in another's expressions of their unique border crossing(s). In class, my small group modeled this for me through their close attention and responsive language to my work.
>
> (McVee et al., 2015, p. 68)

It is very important to note that David felt safe sharing with this group. Additionally, Mary (course instructor) had informed all students ahead of time that they would be sharing their vignettes with their peers. She provided several examples of narratives that students had composed multimodally or in print and reminded students that they should choose to write about what was important to them and be willing to take some risks. Likewise, she encouraged them to set the boundaries they felt comfortable sharing when determining how much personal information they would disclose. David was ready to share his story publicly, but some individuals who identify as LGBTQ may not wish to openly discuss their sexual identity. This is a reminder that a key element of dialogic classrooms is safety and respect (Boyd & Tochelli, 2015). These are key elements of a classroom that promotes "reverent listening" (see Chapter 6, Appendix A).

Veronica's Story

Part of what David wrote about in his narrative vignette was his own internal knowledge that even what some people would consider mere slang, "That's so gay!" was hurtful. It is hurtful when individuals are fearful and are silenced from speaking back against such remarks. Veronica's story is an interesting contrast with David's because her story, in part, revolves around people perceiving her as different. In an end-of-semester written reflection, she described how culture is often seen as something that resides in others and is something "exotic."

> If I had a dollar for every time I was told I looked "exotic" [because of my biracial features], I would be a millionaire. When I entered this literacy and culture class for the first time, I thought that I could use my partial Asian background to my advantage. Throughout my academic career I had been celebrated as a student who came from a "culturally diverse background"

and could supply something other than a White homogenous perspective, and I was comfortable talking about culture; it was essentially my comfort zone. . . .

Because I had lived my entire life being told that I was culturally diverse and exotic looking compared to my Caucasian classmates, I had developed some kind of superiority complex about my cultural knowledge. I was on a cultural power trip, and my positioning during group discussions and thinking was narrow and close-minded . . . possessing a "self-opposed to others position" (McVee, Baldassarre, & Bailey, 2004). This biased my thinking when listening to other classmates and poisoned my understanding of what my peers were saying. I couldn't possibly understand how these very homogenous White-looking peers of mine could have anything of importance to say about culture. McDermott writes that "culture can disable" (1995, p. 327), and I meant to disable the classmates around me with what I perceived to be my culturally diverse superiority. What I should have been doing rather than coming from a place of power was to start listening more."

Veronica continued her writing to describe how she actually experienced a real dialogue and new learning as she met with her peers, Morgan and Mariah, to discuss her narrative with them, and, importantly, as she began to listen to them and other classmates. Veronica described how Morgan's stories about her Greek grandparents seemed familiar to her own stories about her Japanese grandmother, but in a similar fashion she noted what was different:

However I found her [Morgan's] stories about twin culture much more interesting. Morgan spoke about her experiences in high school and college with her twin sister with such enthusiasm that I can recall each story vividly. Morgan's stories about twin culture didn't involve race or ethnicity, yet strangers and friends alike treated her differently because she had a sister who looked like her. Morgan's stories about twin culture were compelling—her identity was defined at face value as a twin, but once she went to college, she became a sole individual, completely changing her identity. This was the kind of first-hand knowledge that I could have never known without her help, and I was grateful to listen and learn all about it. This was the moment that had proven to me that culture encompassed many facets of life, not just the color of one's skin, the language they spoke or foreign relatives.

Veronica's writing continued to document her thinking in ways that demonstrated an empathic stance toward others. Drawing upon Ladson-Billings's (2006) assertion that many times White students "describe themselves as having 'no culture' or being 'just regular'" (Ladson-Billings, p. 107), Veronica wrote that "Students should be taught to understand that culture doesn't necessarily have to be tied to race; culture can also include environment, socio-economic status, and particular ways of thinking, talking, and acting." Whereas Veronica had always found her ethnic and cultural backgrounds provided an easy entry point for conversations about diversity, she realized that other students had not easily found such entry points. She even thought back to high school discussions and wondered if such conversations were "boring and unappealing" because some of her peers had felt their own backgrounds seemed "lacking in culture and diversity." She wrote that it was possible that her high school peers, who were mostly White, may have "felt that they lacked any kind of personal contribution to the discussions at hand, and their power of culture was taken from them." Veronica linked these ideas to Mariah, another group member who had struggled with her vignette. Veronica observed:

> During the first couple weeks of classes, Mariah had felt as though her vignette wasn't exciting or interesting when compared to stories provided by Morgan and myself. She [Mariah] stated that she didn't have any foreign relatives and instead chose to write about a classroom cultural experience. Like the students in Ladson-Billings's article, Mariah felt as though she too was lacking in culture. Although Mariah may have felt as though her story was not 'cultural' enough to share, our vignette group made sure to encourage her story and was careful not to disenfranchise Mariah's experience, which was just as important as any ethnic example we could have shared.
>
> Enciso (1994) points out that as teachers, it is especially important to 'keep in mind that cultural knowledge is everywhere and always a part of how we interpret the world and our place in it' (p. 522). This not only teaches students to value their own roots but to create cultural lessons that are class inclusive and community specific; teaching students that culture is a commonality we share, not something to be hoarded like gold. Once students realize that they possess the power of culture, teachers and students can 'be more cognizant and of their active involvement in the process of determining who they are in our society.'
>
> (Enciso, 1994, p. 533)

Veronica was clear in her writing and course work that she was not replacing her cultural identity with a sense of colorblindness or a misconstrued belief that all students have the same experience. Rather, her realization was that we are not the same. Even in a classroom where all students appear to be the same race, the same ethnicity, or the same social and economic standing, there are still differences that should be valued.

Natalee's Story

Natalee wrote about how reading Karen Hankins's (2003) book, *Teaching Through the Storm*, caused her to rethink a child she had encountered in different student teaching placements. She described one girl who had emotional outbursts similar to some of the children Hankins described. Natalee wrote that initially she had felt pleased with her response to the girl and that her focus had been on her own teacher behavior. But Hankins's text caused Natalee to look at her own behavior in a new light:

> The way that the author handled the outbursts in her classroom made me think back to how I evaluated and handled these situations and what I was thinking when they occurred. I know that I judged the situation and put myself in a selfish position. I was concerned about myself as I dealt with her outburst, hoping that I was doing the right things and that I wouldn't be perceived as someone who couldn't handle situations. After something would happen, I would praise myself for pulling through, and I would feel proud. This is something that I am not completely proud of. Although the author displayed similar feelings to mine of (hoping I was doing the right thing), she displayed the importance of thinking of the child. If I could go back, I would attempt to connect with this student better and try and help her instead of fearing her.

Natalee's multimodal composition for her Book Log was a rectangular poster constructed out of paper and tag board. The poster was a bit like a collage with a multicolored background that framed the edges. Natalee explained that each color in the poster was chosen for a reason:

> Red represents rage, anger and also courage. Pink represents love and friendship. Orange represents distrust, while yellow represents intellect and joy. The color blue represents power and integrity. Black is used to represent death and evil, while White is used to represent goodness and innocence (Color Meaning, 2006). All of these characteristics were displayed in this book through the author, the events, or the children themselves.

In this multicolored border area, Natalee pasted quotes from the text, words, photos, and symbols that represented themes and ideas in the book (Figure 7.2).

This close-up shows how Natalee used a powerful combination of modes (e.g., space, color, image, linguistic text) to communicate meaning. For example, her focus on poverty and the treatment of children is made more potent by the juxtaposition with the image of the isolated child.

At the center of the poster Natalee constructed a maze (Figure 7.3).

The maze represents the challenge that faced Karen Hankins and the children in her classroom. The dotted lines show the clear path from Start to Finish and follow the positive characteristics that Mrs. Hankins enacted in her classroom, such as courage, connecting, hope, and determination. The dead ends are labeled with words that were roadblocks to the classroom community or the children's opportunities to learn. Violence, scheduling, lack of support, anger, and abuse are some of the words that appear here.

FIGURE 7.2 The outer border of Natalee's multimodal composition for *Teaching Through The Storm* (Hankins, 2003). (View in color at marymcvee.com.)

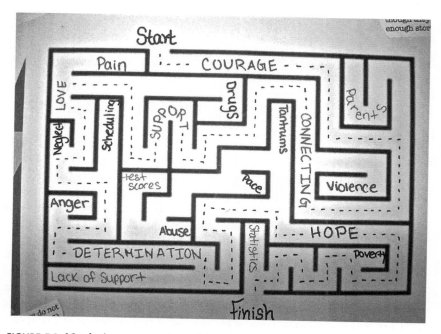

FIGURE 7.3 Natalee's representation of the challenge faced by Hankins and her students in *Teaching Through the Storm* (Hankins, 2003).

It was clear that Natalee felt a deep empathy for the children in Hankins's classroom and for Hankins as a teacher. She concluded her Book Log by writing that she had

> learned the importance of having hope and how important it is to apply all interpretations of this word to the school environment. I also learned the importance of having faith in students, even if the situation seems impossible. I will carry this knowledge with me as I interact with children throughout my life, both in and out of the classroom. ". . . faith is hearing tomorrow's music but . . . hope is dancing to it today."
>
> (Hankins, 2003, p. 150)

Conclusion

A close reading of multicultural text and an authentic response to text are essential for growth and exploration of hot lava topics. Whether writing in traditional academic prose and providing evidence (Karen and Janice) or through multimodal compositions and explaining design choices (David and Natalee) or in face-to-face Book Club discussions, exploring hot lava topics is not an easy task. But, it is a rewarding one. Over many years of interacting with adult students and children, we know that if we take the risk and talk about issues that may be uncomfortable for us, we can learn to listen to others with differing viewpoints.

For Further Reading

Boyd, F.B., & Howe, D.R. (2006). Teaching warriors don't cry with other text types to enhance comprehension. *English Journal, 95*, 61–68.

McEntarfer, H., & McVee, M.B. (2014). 'What are you gay?' Positioning in monologues written and performed by members of a gay–straight alliance. *Linguistics and Education, 25*, 78–89. doi:10.1016/j.linged.2013.09.008

References

Au, K. (1998). Social constructivism and the school literacy learning of students of diverse backgrounds. *Journal of Literacy Research, 30*(2), 297–319.

Boyd, F.B., & Tochelli, A.L. (2015). Designing safe places to talk about contentious topics. In F.B. Boyd & C.H. Brock (Eds.), *Social diversity within multiliteracies: Complexity in teaching and learning* (pp. 89–106). New York: Routledge.

Burbules, N.C. (1993). *Dialogue in teaching: Theory and practice*. New York: Teachers College Press.

Color Meaning. (2006). QSX Software Group. Retrieved from http://www.color-wheel-pro.com/color-meaning.html

Delpit, L. (1988). The silenced dialogue: Power and pedagogy in educating other people's children. *Harvard Educational Review, 58*(3), 280–298.

Enciso, P. (1994). Cultural identity and response to literature: Running lessons from Maniac Magee. *Language Arts, 71*(7), 524–533.

Frankenberg, R. (1993). *White women, race matters: The social construction of whiteness*. Minneapolis, MN: University of Minnesota Press.

Hankins, K. (2003). *Teaching through the storm*. New York: Teachers College Press.

King, J.E. (1991). Dysconscious racism: Ideology, identity, and the miseducation of teachers. *Journal of Negro Education, 60*(2), 133–146.

Ladson-Billings, G. (2006). It's not the culture of poverty, it's the poverty of culture: The problem with teacher education. *Anthropology & Education Quarterly, 37*(2), 104–109.

McIntyre, A. (1997). *Making meaning of whiteness*. New York: State University of New York Press.

McVee, M.B., Baldassarre, M., & Bailey, N.M. (2004). Positioning theory as lens to explore teachers' beliefs about literacy and culture. In C.M. Fairbanks, J. Worthy, B. Maloch, J.V. Hoffman, & D.L. Schallert (Eds.), *53rd National Reading Conference Yearbook* (pp. 281–295). Oak Creek, WI: National Reading Conference.

McVee, M.B., Fronczak, D., Stainsby, J., & White, C. (2015). White male teachers exploring language, literacy and diversity. In F.B. Boyd & C.H. Brock (Eds.), *Social diversity within multiliteracies: Complexity in Teaching and learning* (pp. 58–73). New York: Routledge.

Shanahan, L.E., McVee, M.B., Schiller, J.A., Tynan, E.A., D'Abate, R.L., Flury-Kashmanian, C.M., . . . & Hayden, H.E. (2013). Supporting struggling readers and literacy clinicians through reflective video pedagogy. In E.T. Ortlieb & E.H. Cheek, Jr. (Eds.), *Advanced literacy practices: From the clinic to the classroom literacy* (Vol. 2). Bingley, UK: Emerald Group Publishing.

8

ALL THE STORIES WE HAVE YET TO HEAR

REFLECTION QUESTIONS

1. Describe a teacher who made a positive impact on your life.
2. What was important about that teacher?
3. What did you learn from her/him?
4. How did this teacher inspire you?

Veteran educator Rita Pierson reminds us that children and youth respond best when they have a relationship with their teachers. In "Every Kid Needs a Champion" (2013, https://www.ted.com/talks/rita_pierson_every_kid_needs_a_champion), Pierson uses humor, joy, and story to refocus educators on the needs of kids. Her observation that teachers should seek understanding first—before we seek to be understood—is a reminder of the importance of listening in building relationships. Pierson delivers a powerful message for educators:

> How powerful would our world be if we had kids who were not afraid to take risks and who were not afraid to think and who had a champion? Every child deserves a champion, an adult who will never give up on them, who understands the power of connection and insists that they become the best that they can possibly be.

What is impressive about Pierson and the many other teachers similar to her is that they see opportunity where others see failure. Pierson uses the example of a child who earned a 2 out of 20 on a quiz. When Pierson put a smiley face on the paper, the child was confused and asked: "Is this an F?" Pierson responded, "Yes."

As a teacher, Mrs. Pierson is fully cognizant that this child had deficits—a 2 out of 20 is not acceptable. She is honest in her statement that helping kids who have many gaps in their knowledge and growing that knowledge to where it needs to be is a lot of "hard work." But, Pierson is also cognizant of a child's spirit. Viewing a child as only his deficits means ignoring all the potential growth that could be taking place. In Pierson's eyes, here was a child who had the potential to get 18 more correct answers the next time around, and as a teacher Pierson was determined to help him reach that goal. In sum, we gain nothing by telling children only what they are failing to do. We gain everything by showing them what they can do better and how they can grow. We gain by listening.

Working to Counter Deficit Models of Students and Teachers

The same principles that apply to teaching children often apply to teaching teachers: We gain nothing by telling teachers only what they are failing to do. We gain everything by showing them what they can do better and how they can grow. We gain by listening.

The teachers with whom we have worked in our careers as teacher educators are those teachers most representative of the teaching cohort in the United States. They have been predominantly White, female, monolingual, and from middle-class suburban backgrounds. While our examples in this text come from a US context, we know that the US is not unique. There are many countries where scholars and teacher educators have wrestled with how to assist predominantly White, monolingual English-speaking teachers in meeting the needs of children who are culturally, ethnically, and linguistically diverse. We are heartened by the surge of interest that teacher educators and researchers have demonstrated in helping teachers think about the needs of all children over the past two decades.

Several scholars have aptly pointed out that teacher educators who work with predominantly White teachers often reproduce the very deficit model they are attempting to help their inservice and preservice teachers to critique (e.g., McCarthy, 2003; Lensmire, 2010). Rather than treating educators as individuals with localized and unique experiences to build upon, Lowenstein (2009) argues that multicultural teacher education often centers the problem on

> a widely held and often unexamined conceptualization of White teacher candidates as deficient learners about issues of diversity in multicultural teacher education. In this view, teacher candidates are learners who lack resources or who have deficient knowledge or experience from which to build when it comes to learning about these issues. (p. 163)

This is why this book has stressed examples of teachers and teacher candidates as learners who are contending with ideas. We have pointed out how these learners are struggling and what we can learn together by looking at those examples. We believe that all educators, no matter how experienced, can benefit from participating in such dialogue. We recognize that in our own personal and professional lives, we have direct experiences (sometimes painful experiences) of discrimination based on gender, class, and race. However, many teachers have not had these direct experiences, but they do have lived experience to build upon. Our goal in this book is to help open up dialogic spaces where teachers can explore the often-contentious issues of identity and values that are intertwined with "hot lava" topics, regardless of previous experiences.

Reframing Our Language and Positions: Challenges We All Share

Where we have written "educators" or "teachers" in this book, we are addressing ourselves as researchers/teacher educators and likewise we are addressing our colleagues in the field. The quote from Cochran-Smith (1995) that opened the introductory chapter of this book could be revised as:

> **Teachers, teacher educators, and researchers** need opportunities to examine much of what is usually unexamined in the tightly braided relationships of language, culture, and power in schools and schooling.

This assertion raises two key points:

1. *All* of us have views, values, and beliefs we need to examine; teacher educators and scholars are not exempt.
2. Creating opportunities to consider the relationships between literacy, language, and culture is a different approach than presenting "issues of diversity" as the problem to be solved.

An exchange between us (Mary and Fenice) illustrates these points. In drafting this text, at one point Fenice challenged Mary's use of the phrase "issues of diversity" because this usage indirectly positions diversity as *the* problem. Fenice had been pondering the use of the phrase in her own work around issues of multiliteracies (see Boyd & Brock, 2015). This subtle, but very important, discourse shift led Mary to ruminate more deeply about how she was framing this issue within her writing and teaching. Framing diversity around "issues" or "problems" might suggest that diversity itself is the problem. Such framing could be viewed as an example of dysconscious racism as discussed in Chapter 7.

This example does not contain the dramatic epiphany or conversion moment that is often written about in the literature. Mary has considerable experience in various cultures, through studies around explorations of language, literacy, culture, and diversity, and she has taught in settings that foreground explorations of language and literacy for nearly 30 years. But, we share this example to demonstrate that even someone who has considerable experience can still be prompted to think more deeply about her own stance toward diversity, and how language-in-use points to distinctions that are often subtle, but critical nonetheless. All of us—teachers, teacher educators, administrators, scholars, and other educational professionals—must consider our positions as related to the diverse contexts and learners in our educational systems. This is a journey rather than an end point; there is always room for new exploration.

All and *always* are two important words that mark this journey. The journey applies to all of us. Just as Mary was prompted to rethink the deeper positions underlying her talk, as an African American woman Fenice too continues to engage in her own explorations. Fenice's learning and thinking has continued to evolve across time. Even though Fenice is considered a minority within the larger US context and her lived experiences reflect the historical, social, and cultural nuances of that context, she must also engage in related explorations of herself and her views of literacy, language, and culture. As we finalized this manuscript, Fenice was preparing for an extended visit to work with educators and researchers in Australia. She fully expects that crossing cultural (and linguistic!) borders will create displacement spaces for her to further her learning related to literacy, language, and culture. Without a doubt, all learners bring something very different to the table, but everyone has something to gain and to learn on the journey.

This journey should help teachers and teacher educators consistently seek new destinations and challenges. Even if our insights are those small, nuanced bursts of recognition rather than true epiphanies, all of us should be wary of thinking we have truly arrived and have no more left to learn. We must also monitor our language-in-use. Because language both constructs and represents our perceived realities, discourse matters. But we should be mindful too that if we focus only on *what* we say, we change only the surface representation. Politically correct talk often functions in this manner. For example, when making a public statement, the CEO of a corporation might use gender-inclusive language to make clear that women are valued in the corporate workplace, but it is the "small stories" (Bamberg & Georgakopoulou, 2008) that make up our day-to-day reality. If language shift is not linked to deeper considerations of position and value, shifting talk around gender to be "politically correct"—that is, it will keep up the appearance of including women as equal partners—will not change deeper power structures. Politically correct speech is an outward marker and may be an important first step toward awareness, but the deeper changes and more challenging shifts are those we face internally. These are shifts not only in the words we use, but to the stories we tell about others and ultimately, about ourselves.

Shifting Demographics and Changing Societies

In this book we have argued that cultural explorations are not merely important, they are essential. In addition to the small stories we share on a daily basis, there is also a global story unfolding. Sadly, while the world has become more globally connected, many nations have found persistent problems related to race, gender, class, mother tongue, poverty, and schooling success (or lack of success). World migration figures have grown steadily, for example, increasing from 154 million in 1990 to 231 million in 2013 (UN-DESA & OECD, 2013). This unprecedented migration—some by choice, much due to ethnic or religious conflict or economic necessity—is profoundly changing societies that were already experiencing demographic shifts. Countries such as Australia, the US, Canada, the UK, and other traditionally White majority countries are experiencing greater diversity. Newcomers in many societies are adding to the demographic shifts that were already underway. For example, in the United Kingdom, White Britons are predicted to become the minority by 2070 (White Britons, 'Will Be Minority', 2013). In the United States, by mid-century the White majority is predicted to shift to a White minority (Yen, 2013).

These population shifts when coupled with rapidly changing technologies and social change make it imperative that teachers and other school professionals come to understand how their lived histories affect their choices in framing literacy, culture, language, teaching, and learning. Educators need to be cognizant of how student identities and histories can influence facets of literacy teaching and learning. These concerns transcend national boundaries.

Consider that despite the differences in their educational systems and policies, Australia, Canada, the UK, and the US have all expressed concerns about children who do not succeed in schooling or, put another way, children for whom the educational system is failing. Children in middle- or upper-class families, children who are native speakers of their country's national or dominant language, and children who are White are more likely to be successful in schooling and to complete their education than children of color, nonnative speakers of French or English, or indigenous minorities. While none of these countries practice *de jure* segregation (segregation enforced by law), there is increasing concern, particularly in the US with its history of segregation, of *de facto* segregation (segregation brought about by history or poverty or other factors). In many countries the poor, immigrants, and non-White populations are clustered into neighborhoods that occasionally erupt in violence as people, particularly the young, express their feelings of injustice and frustration. We point this out not to condemn these countries or communities but to note that racism, poverty, and opportunity are intertwined. Education, particularly literacy, has long been considered a gateway to accessing better opportunities for one's self and one's children. Addressing these opportunity gaps is critical to addressing the inequities that exist across the different and diverse groups in our society.

In the big picture, the big story, diversity itself presents an opportunity. As the New London Group says, "To this end, cultural and linguistic diversity is a classroom resource just as powerfully as it is a social resource in the formation of new civic spaces and new notions of citizenship" (New London Group, 2000, p. 15).

One of the ways we can tap into and draw strength from this diversity is by sharing our stories, whether composed in writing, spoken aloud, through multimodal digital works, or through the creative arts. Stories are the stuff of connection. From our earliest relationships with caregivers and family to the relationships that we form as adults, stories are the glue that connects us together. It seems fitting, then, that we (Fenice and Mary) end this book where we began, with our own stories.

More Stories to Tell

There are many stories that we could have chosen to tell here, but we chose the stories below for particular reasons. Mary first considered writing about how after university she had traveled to China to teach English or more recent adventures in raising her three biracial children. But she wanted to revisit that initial experience of crossing the invisible borders of social and economic class that were reflected in continuing her education by going to college. Her story is about invisible or less visible borders of economic class. In contrast, Fenice wanted to share a story where she had crossed physical, geographic, cultural, and social borders in a dramatic way. She easily could have written about her shift from southern state North Carolina to Michigan, where she enrolled in a doctoral program, or about other experiences she had while traveling in the US, even within her home state, or as far away as Africa. But instead she chose to write about an experience that gave her a unique insight into some of what English language learners or new immigrants might feel in their schooling when they must cross boundaries.

Fenice's Story

About 10 years ago I visited Macedonia as a volunteer and literacy expert on behalf of the International Reading Association (IRA, now International Literacy Association). IRA and USAID (United States Agency for International Development) had a collaborative grant to provide professional development to Macedonian high school teachers working in vocational schools. The purpose was to refocus teachers' pedagogical skills so they would become more student centered. This professional development initiative took place countrywide, requiring literacy experts to make multiple trips to Macedonia. The experience described below took place on my third or fourth visit to Macedonia.

One morning I had to be at a high school to observe several teachers to see how they were implementing what they had learned during the professional development seminars that my colleagues and I facilitated. My translator was not able to pick me up because she had to take her children to school, so she asked me to take a taxi and meet her there. The school was about a 30-minute ride away from the bed and breakfast where my colleagues and I were staying. Because I was a bit nervous about traveling without my translator, I asked the receptionist working that morning to write down the name of the school in Cyrillic so I could give it to the taxi cab driver. When I slid into the back seat of the taxi, I gave the name of the school to him. He didn't say anything to me, but appeared to know where I needed to go by the nod of his head. (Some bodily gestures are universal.) The trip to the school was uneventful, but I did enjoy the ride and looking at the beautiful, but unfamiliar, terrain. I remember thinking about what a privilege it was for me to be able to participate in such an important professional development initiative, and that it would be an experience forever in my memory. We arrived at the school safely. I paid the driver, and got out of the taxi.

It is important to remember that when I started this story, I said that I was scheduled to observe teachers at a high school (or what the Macedonians call "secondary school"). As I was walking toward the school's entrance, I saw parents zip past me holding the hands of these "little people." When I saw those very young children coming to school, I realized right away that I was in trouble! (The word that I said to myself after the word "OH" isn't appropriate to tell you here!) I looked toward the street, but of course, the cab had left. As I entered the building, I saw a young girl sitting at a desk right by the entrance; she looked to be around 11 or 12 years old. I said, "Hi. Do you speak English?" She gestured with her hand by holding it out flat and tilting it from one side to another in a "so-so" move and replied, "A little bit." I asked if she would direct me to the principal's office. She took me to what appeared to be a teachers' lounge. There were several people in the room, talking and smoking cigarettes. One woman (who I assumed to be a teacher) said to me, in Macedonian, "Who are you and what are you doing here?" (The young girl translated for me!) I had to chuckle to myself at this woman's question because I too wanted to know what I was doing there! I explained the situation as the young girl translated. The teacher was very helpful. She knew what school I was supposed to be visiting—that piece of paper with the address came in handy. The teacher immediately called a taxi to the school and walked with me out to the taxi and told him in Macedonian where I was to be dropped off.

I don't know if I can convey in this narrative the feelings of panic and alarm that came over me before this mistake was straightened out. I was on my own and at the wrong school. I didn't speak one word of the language (well, I had learned to say hello—*Zdravo!*). Some Macedonians speak English, but most did not at the time. During our first development seminar with the Macedonian teachers, I remember one teacher telling me how he wished that he could speak English.

I didn't know where I was or how to get to the right school. My translator was probably just arriving at the high school waiting for me, and I was going to be late for my observations. My translator would more than likely be worried about me, and I didn't have any way to contact her to let her know I was lost. The questions and anxiety level rose with each passing moment.

You might be wondering why the taxi took me to the wrong school in the first place. I did have an address. Well, little did I know that in Macedonia, some schools have the exact same name, so the taxi driver had dropped me off at the school with the name that was written down. Initially, I was not exactly sure if the receptionist at the bed and breakfast wrote down the correct address or not. I do remember showing the taxi driver the schedule that was given to me. The schedule definitely had the name of the school if not the address. The glitch here was that there was a private elementary school and a public high school with exactly the same name in approximately the same vicinity, thus, the confusion.

What's the point of my final story? Well, this border-crossing experience is not a story about how I had never been out of my comfort zone or in unfamiliar contexts. There were lots of times I had been out of my comfort zone even in the US. When I went to Michigan State University to work on my Ph.D., for example, I remember feeling awkward in my first class because I was the only African American student. Out of all my years of going to school, that was the first time that I was the only Black student in the class. Likewise, I remember the first time that I took a trip to the western part of North Carolina, my home state where I was born and raised. I was a young adult in my early twenties and had never been on the opposite end of NC. There are beautiful tall mountains everywhere. Additionally, there were different people with different southern accents. The "locals" looked at my friends and me as if we had two heads! I could tell that they knew we were not from Boone, NC, and I felt awkward and displaced. And when I went to Macedonia, it wasn't my first time traveling to a different country either. I'd been to several other places around the world. In fact, before Macedonia, I had visited two African nations, and although I saw a "sea of Black people" everywhere I looked, people who were educated and running the country, and people who were uneducated and working as hotel servants and farmers, that feeling of displacement was there with me in Zimbabwe and South Africa, too. So what was it about this particular border-crossing experience in Macedonia that was so different?

Although I've had many border-crossing experiences related to race, this Macedonian incident, for me, wasn't about race. Yes, I definitely presented a visual difference while there. There are no Black people in Macedonia—at least there weren't when I was there. But this border crossing was more about *my* inability to communicate effectively, to say to people in their home language, "Hi. I'm lost! Will you please help me?"

When I arrived at the wrong school in Macedonia, I was a long, long way from Warrenton, NC, both geographically and professionally. I was on my way to conduct teacher observations as an "expert" in the field. I was making a contribution to this professional development initiative and was honored to be a part of it. But at this particular point and time, my expertise to articulate my thinking, and thus my confidence level, was surely disrupted. I have often thought about children who enter US schools without speaking or have no knowledge of the English language—typically the only language of instruction! What must they be feeling? And how, when all the odds appear to be stacked against them, do they survive?

My Macedonian border crossing really brought that reality home for me. I was placed in a position where I was challenged to think about what to do to survive because I didn't speak the language.

Clearly, my experiences as a well-educated adult who had travelled before are not the same as a child who does not speak English in an English-speaking country or a youth who is a recent immigrant who has not had formal schooling and now must attend school. These children face more hurdles with fewer resources than I had acquired. The point is that my experience, while not the same, was an experience I could use to build upon and an experience that could help me to think empathetically about others. These are skills I have been able to put into practice in recent work back home in the US, where for the last few years I have had the privilege of working with a high school where 70% of the student population speak more than 42 languages. These children attend what the state has designated a "failing school" because they do not pass state tests. But many of the youth in this school are recent immigrants, many are refugees, and many are students with interrupted formal schooling (sometimes called "SIFE" students). They cross visible and invisible borders on a daily basis. Keeping my own experiences with border crossings in mind has assisted me as I have worked with school administrators, teachers, and youth.

Mary's Story

I've been pondering something that Rita Pierson said in her talk that we referred in the beginning of this chapter about how children won't learn from people they don't like. As a student I had many teachers whom I really liked. Mrs. Martin taught me to read and was gentle with me, a very shy girl who once cried in Mrs. Martin's first grade class because I did not have a pencil! Mrs. Dix, my third grade teacher, was kind and energetic, making sure I was challenged in my reading and writing. She was the first teacher to read one of my stories out loud, which made me feel like a real author. My science teacher Mr. Hahn was hysterically fun, full of antics, but also very demanding, and although he wanted me to be a doctor and not a writer, his support for me as a learner gave me confidence. Mrs. Rusher was encouraging, positive, and challenged me to challenge myself by playing with different writing styles and learning from authors whom I admired, like Ray Bradbury. I really liked all of these teachers. But I also had a professor in college, Professor Justman. I guess I liked Professor Justman—I had several classes with him, but I am not certain that "like" is the right word, perhaps respect is more appropriate. To be honest, I found Professor Justman intimidating.

In my opening narrative for this book, I wrote about how I was originally placed in a remedial writing class when I first attended university. I'm sure my writing was very poor, so based on that sample, it was probably the correct placement. After all, what had made the biggest impression on me was that panicked feeling that the clock was ticking. But, I had a champion, not in Professor

Justman, but in my advisor Professor Maloney. As an incoming freshman, I had been recommended for the Honors College. I really didn't know what that meant, but anything that had the word "honors" in it had to be good, so I signed on. In the Honors College I was assigned a special freshman advisor (Professor Maloney) and had the option to take smaller courses with full-time faculty (not graduate student teaching assistants or part-time adjuncts). Phil Maloney looked at my writing placement test, asked me questions about where I went to school, consulted my academic transcripts, and determined that I should take basic English composition through the Honors College with Professor Justman. At the time, this all seemed relatively arbitrary to me since I had "failed" the placement test. Since that time, I have often wondered how my life would have been different if Professor Maloney had been too busy or too distracted to look at my files. Where would I have learned to write? Or would I have learned to write well?

Writing had always been my dream, but I found that being passionate about something was not the same as being good at it. Professor Justman was a small man with frizzy hair and a falcon's sharp features. The first day of class he announced, "I reserve the right to ask anyone to leave this course. If your writing is not up to my expectations, you will be asked to leave." These were words I heard with dread. It was as if Professor Justman already knew I was an imposter.

Professor Justman believed that we would not learn to write well or construct powerful arguments in writing if we did not read and understand great writing and how it worked. We read from a broad selection of authors. Some of those I remember were writings as disparate as Martin Luther King, Jr. (*Letter from Birmingham Jail*, published in 1963) and Mary Wollstonecraft (excerpts from *A Vindication of the Rights of Woman*, published in 1792). We were expected to read deeply and carefully—a true close reading of the text—to orally express and articulate ideas together as a class, and then construct an essay responding to or exploring a particular idea. Professor Justman was direct in his criticism of our writing ("awkward," "unclear," "word choice," "need example") but also in his praise ("well said," "good example"). He followed these comments with other directed and specific feedback. His comments were not kind, but they were fair. In each class, he read excerpts of our class papers that he felt typified excellent writing. And, he did not spare us from examples of our writing that did not work, but he helped to show us why the writing did not work and how to improve it. His comments were never meant to personally demean a student or for Professor Justman to demonstrate his own position of power. Professor Justman used his comments to teach and to show us the power of writing and the power of a well-constructed argument articulated with "simplicity, clarity, and force."

In that first class, I do not remember talking very much; I lacked confidence and was scared. The kids who had confidence sat at the seminar tables that were closest to where Professor Justman sat or stood near the green chalkboard at the front of the small seminar room. The students who sat at the seminar tables were those who seemed to participate most. They made bold arguments and seemed to speak eloquently and with authority. Most of them came from high schools in Montana's largest cities—Great Falls, Billings, or Missoula—or from cities out of state. These kids wore preppy outfits that marked their economic status as children of professionals; I wore cowboy boots, wranglers, and a leather belt with "MARY" tooled across the back. I sat with the kids on the outer rim of the room where desks ran along the back wall. At the beginning of the semester, the back-row students were much more like spectators than participants. We were kids who mostly came from rural Montana or other small towns—my college roommate Jewell who was from a small town in Alaska sat next to me.

At the time, these distinctions (town kids vs. country kids) seemed like natural distinctions to me—they had been part of my earliest days in school where social groups often divided naturally along "bus kids" and "town kids." But as the semester progressed, some things changed. I noticed that one young man and one young woman who had been most outspoken and self-assured (as I recollect both were from the largest high school in the state) had stopped coming to class. In talking to these students outside of class, they spoke bitterly and condescendingly about Professor Justman. The young man said, "He told me that I wasn't doing quality work. I think my teachers at ___ High School know what quality work is, and they never told me that. I always got straight As. I wasn't learning anything in this class anyway." Whether it was right or not, those of us who toughed it out that semester felt vindicated, especially Jewell. Jewell had struggled more than I with the course, but Professor Justman had met with her many times outside of class and worked with her on her writing. She managed to meet the benchmark through hard work. There was a lesson in that too because in looking back, I think it is very likely that our classmates from larger schools were better prepared because they had more opportunities in their larger cities and high schools. Hard work trumped prior experience. Our peers from some geographic locations certainly acted as if they were entitled to a college degree, but Professor Justman won my admiration for making it clear that all of us were *earning* an education; we would have to work for our success.

Until I heard Rita Pierson's talk, I hadn't really thought about liking or not liking Professor Justman. Over the years, especially as I have realized how much of my writing ability had its genesis in that freshman composition seminar, my appreciation for that first experience has only increased. All those years ago Professor Justman was an intimidating figure. More than liking him, I think I respected him. He seemed like a fair teacher, but also a responsible teacher. He didn't just tell us when we wrote badly constructed prose; he told us what to do to make it better. He didn't just set a high standard; he helped us meet the standard if we were willing to listen. There was power too in the readings he chose to have us study and discuss. I can't recall all that we read, but those two pieces that I do recall (King and Wollstonecraft) were not only powerfully written arguments, they were arguments aimed at communicating messages of social justice for all peoples.

Professor Justman could have easily looked at the row of us around the edge of the room and dismissed us as "those kids" whose working-class roots hadn't really prepared them for college, but he never did that. If we were willing to work, he was willing to work with us. It has now been more than 30 years since I sat in that classroom, but whenever I write, Professor Justman's critique and admonishments are there in the margins and keep me searching out awkward sentences, poor word choice, and inadequate examples. He is not the only teacher who helped me on my journey—I wish I could write about everyone who helped me—but his writing instruction gave me access to the academic world or the "culture of power" (Delpit, 1988, p. 282) that was used to measure academic success. This access to the culture of power has not only allowed me to pursue academic achievements, but has provided a stepping stone that gave me access to more opportunities and choices.

Conclusion

In conclusion, teachers and teacher educators and the positions they enact have a profound influence on the lives of those they teach, and because of this, teachers have an immensely important role to play in addressing issues of inequity and creating sustained change within schools. At a time where the focus in schools has been on reforming standards, implementing new curricula, and increasing accountability and testing from the top down, it seems essential to vocalize support for teachers.

Individual teachers, their beliefs, and their instructional choices matter to students. It is unlikely that ten years from now today's students will reflect back on which Common Core State Standard most influenced their learning, but it is extremely likely that today's students will ruminate on which teachers most strongly, passionately, and positively influenced their development and love of learning in powerful ways. There is a story yet to be created by you and your students. What story would you help them hear? What story would you help them tell?

References

Bamberg, M., & Georgakopoulou, A. (2008). Small stories as a new perspective in narrative and identity analysis. *Text and Talk, 28*(3), 377–396.

Boyd, F.B., & Brock, C.H. (Eds.). (2015). *Social diversity within multiliteracies: Complexity in teaching and learning.* New York: Routledge.

Cochran-Smith, M. (1995). Color blindness and basket making are not the answers: Confronting the dilemmas of race, culture, and language diversity in teacher education. *American Educational Research Journal, 32*(3), 493–522.

Delpit, L. (1988). The silenced dialogue: Power and pedagogy in educating other people's children. *Harvard Educational Review, 58*(3), 280–298.

King, M. L., Jr. (1963). Letter from Birmingham Jail. Retrieved from https://kinginstitute. stanford.edu/king-papers/documents/letter-birmingham-jail

Lensmire, T.J. (2010). Ambivalent white racial identities: Fear and elusive innocence. *Race Ethnicity and Education, 13*(2), 159–172. doi:10.1080/13613321003751577.

Lowenstein., K.L. (2009). The work of multicultural teacher education: Reconceptualizing White teacher candidates as learners. *Review of Educational Research, 79*(1), 163–196.

McCarthy, C. (2003). Contradictions of power and identity: Whiteness studies and the call of teacher education. *International Journal of Qualitative Studies in Education, 16*(1), 127–133.

New London Group. (2000). A pedagogy of multiliteracies: Designing social futures. In B. Cope & M. Kalantzis (Eds.), *Multiliteracies: Literacy learning and the design of social futures* (pp. 9–37). New York: Routledge.

Pierson, R. (2013, May). Rita Pierson: Every kid needs a champion. [Video file]. Retrieved from https://www.ted.com/talks/rita_pierson_every_kid_needs_a_champion#t-4205

UN-DESA & OECD (United Nations Department of Economic and Social Affairs & Organisation for Economic Co-operation and Development). (2013, October). World migration figures. Retrieved from http://www.oecd.org/els/mig/World-Migration-in-Figures.pdf

White Britons 'will be minority' before 2070, says professor. (2013, May 2). *The Independent.* Retrieved from http://www.independent.co.uk/news/uk/home-news/white-britons-will-be-minority-before-2070-says-professor-8600262.html

Wollstonecraft, M. (1792). A Vindication of the rights of women with strictures on political and moral subjects. Retrieved from http://www.bartleby.com/144/

Yen, H. (2013, June 13). Census: White majority in U.S. gone by 2043. [NBC News story]. Retrieved from http://usnews.nbcnews.com/_news/2013/06/13/18934111-census-white-majority-in-us-gone-by-2043

CONTRIBUTORS

Fenice B. Boyd is Associate Professor, Literacy, Graduate School of Education, University at Buffalo, SUNY, USA.

James R. Gavelek is an Associate Professor at the University of Illinois at Chicago. His scholarly interests focus on the role of language and other embodied semiotic processes in understanding the development of mind, rethinking teaching, learning, and school curriculum.

Mary B. McVee is Associate Professor, Literacy, and Director of the Center for Literacy and Reading Instruction, Graduate School of Education, University at Buffalo, SUNY, USA.

Taffy E. Raphael is a Professor at the University of Illinois at Chicago, and Co-founder and President of SchoolRise, LLC. Her research interests include strategy instruction in comprehension and writing, and frameworks for literacy curriculum and instruction (e.g. Book Club Plus).

Lisa Roof is a doctoral candidate at the University of Buffalo, SUNY. Her research focuses on multimodality, gesture, and identity. She is currently completing an ethnographic study of immigrant Burmese adolescents and their identity narratives.

INDEX